I0817260

365 Daily Devotions for Couples

BroadStreet
PUBLISHING

BroadStreet Publishing Group, LLC.
Savage, Minnesota, USA
Broadstreetpublishing.com

A Little We Time with God

9781424571529
9781424571536 eBook

Compiled and edited by Natasha Marcellus.

Typesetting and design by Garborg Design Works | garborgdesign.com
Editorial services by Michelle Winger | literallyprecise.com

Printed in China.

26 27 28 29 30 31 32 7 6 5 4 3 2 1

Two are better than one because they have a good reward for their efforts.

Ecclesiastes 4:9 CSB

INTRODUCTION

Marriage is a sacred union: a daily invitation to love, grow, forgive, and walk together in faith. In the whirlwind of responsibilities, routines, and distractions, it's easy to lose sight of the spiritual bond that anchors your relationship.

A Little We Time with God invites couples to pause together each day, connect with God, and strengthen their relationship from the inside out. In each entry you'll find a Scriptures to anchor your marriage in truth, a short devotion to inspire heartfelt connection, and a guided prayer to invite God into your everyday life.

Whether you're newly married or seasoned in love, this book helps you grow closer to each other and to the one who brought you together. Create a sacred rhythm of togetherness and discover the power of "we" time with God.

JANUARY

Be completely humble and gentle; be patient, bearing with one another in love. Make every effort to keep the unity of the Spirit through the bond of peace.

Ephesians 4:2-3 NIV

JANUARY 1

If any of you lacks wisdom, let him ask God, who gives generously to all without reproach, and it will be given him.

James 1:5 ESV

God loves to give his children wisdom. He loves to guide us through each of our days, and he loves when we depend on him. He is ready to equip us no matter what we are facing. When we ask him for help, he readily tells us what to do. He has the answers we need, and he does not hide them from us.

Let dependence on God be the foundation of your marriage. It doesn't matter how long you've been married. There will never be a point when you are better off figuring it out on your own. Run to the Lord and ask him for guidance in every situation. Lean on him together and be determined to follow his instructions rather than your own plans and ideas.

How can you practice dependence on God in your marriage today?

UNITY IN MARRIAGE

Make my joy complete by being of the same mind, maintaining the same love, united in spirit, intent on one purpose.

PHILIPPIANS 2:2 NASB

For believers to be united in love, we must let Christ dwell in us richly. As we follow his lead, we will display the same beautiful disposition that he had during his earthly life. It is all the more important for married couples to strive toward being like-minded and united in love and purpose. They are joined as one and are lifelong partners in the work of the gospel.

Together with your spouse, commit to growing and maturing in your faith. Only as you are transformed into the likeness of Christ, by the power of the Holy Spirit, will you be able to discern what is of God and display it in your lives.

In what ways can you encourage each other to grow in Christ this week?

NO FEAR

There is no fear in love, but perfect love drives out fear, because fear involves punishment, and the one who fears is not perfected in love.

1 John 4:18 NASB

When we are confident of God's love for us, we won't be ruled by shame, embarrassment, or fear. Those things take over our minds when we are constantly worried about God's punishment or disapproval. Scripture reminds us that we are not meant to live that way. We are meant to be governed by love.

Has shame, fear, pride, or embarrassment kept you from greater intimacy as a married couple? There is a better way. As you experience God's perfect love, you will be able to extend it to your spouse. As you become convinced of his kindness, gentleness, and overflowing mercy, you will be able to love each other with the same qualities.

What is one area where you can replace fear or shame with God's love in order to deepen your intimacy as a couple?

PROCESS ANGER

Be angry, and do not sin;
ponder in your own hearts on your beds,
and be silent.

PSALM 4:4 ESV

Feeling angry is not a sin, but we are responsible for our actions. Even when wrongs have been done against us, we have the option to do what is right. Approaching a difficult situation with an angry heart in the heat of the moment can lead to regrettable outcomes. However, taking time to think through the matter in a private place can bring clarity, so it is easier to address the offenses in a calm and collected state.

Knowing when to be silent and when to speak demonstrates wisdom and self-control. It takes practice to learn how to process our emotions in a healthy way. Outbursts of anger are harmful, and it's important to create an environment where anger can be managed.

How do each of you process anger? Learn each other's preferences and treat your anger as an opportunity to show up for each other.

KINDNESS OVERFLOW

Show respect for all people: Love the brothers and sisters of God's family, respect God, honor the king.

1 Peter 2:17 NCV

We cannot control other people, but we can control our responses. We do not have to agree with our spouse, friends, or those in leadership over us, but we do have to act in a way that is befitting of a child of God. Showing kindness has more power to soften hearts than criticism or frustration. Love and grace bring about more change than any disrespectful rebuttal or angry confrontation.

Your spouse's failures will hit closer to home than anyone else's. Their shortcomings will feel extra disappointing because of how much they impact you. Remember that kindness and gentleness are the tools God has given you for success. Treating each other with respect and love is more important than proving your point or stubbornly insisting on your own way.

How can you continue to love and respect each other when you disagree or are disappointed?

HIGHER CALLING

"If you love those who love you, what credit is that to you? For even sinners love those who love them. And if you do good to those who do good to you, what credit is that to you? For even sinners do the same."

LUKE 6:32-33 NASB

We naturally gravitate toward relationships that offer us something. We like to love people who love us back and treat us how we want to be treated. We all need healthy and fulfilling relationships in our lives, but God also calls us to consistent and faithful in love. We are meant to love and serve people who do not love us back.

As a married couple, you will likely fail each other at some point. You will each have moments or seasons when you are difficult to love. Remember that God equips you to be faithful. He gives you the strength to love each other well even when one or both of you are struggling. He calls you to love each other consistently despite how difficult it is.

How can you intentionally love each other when it's most difficult?

FORGIVENESS

"When you stand praying, if you hold anything against anyone, forgive them, so that your Father in heaven may forgive you your sins."

MARK 11:25 NIV

We've all been insulted, taken advantage of, rejected, inconvenienced, disappointed, or frustrated. None of us are exempt from experiencing hurt or being let down by other people. Scripture reminds us that it's our responsibility to give our hurt to God. Forgiveness is not contingent upon apologies and perfect reconciliations.

God empowers you to forgive even when the situation doesn't look how you want. God is capable of comforting you and healing your heart regardless of how the other person responds. Give him your offenses and he will be faithful to mend what is broken.

Is your willingness to forgive each other dependent on your actions or God's faithfulness?

ASK FOR HELP

"Stand up in the presence of the aged, show respect for the elderly and revere your God. I am the LORD."

LEVITICUS 19:32 NIV

A lot can be learned from those who have walked before us. Asking for wisdom and insight from others who have been married longer can offer great benefits to our marriages. So often we feel like we must rely on our own strength and hide our problems when we should be asking for help.

God has surrounded you with others who have testimonies of their own. It would be to your advantage to find those who are older and wiser, and who have spent years walking with God throughout their marriage. Respecting those who have age and experience on their side and revering God and his Word go hand in hand with growing in wisdom. Your marriage will be better off if you open your ears and hearts to listen and learn.

Do you know anyone who has had a long and godly marriage? Ask them what advice they would offer.

FROM THE OVERFLOW

Each one of you also must love his wife as he loves himself, and the wife must respect her husband.

EPHESIANS 5:33 NIV

Love and respect are basic desires of every human. It is easy to fall into the trap of withholding one or the other from our spouses as a way of controlling them or trying to force change. God asks us to do things differently. His love for us is unending. He does not withhold his love even when we experience the consequences of our own actions.

You have been told to love and respect each other. You can do this because of the incredible love God has shown you. You can highly esteem each other every day because of what God has done for you. Your mutual love and respect is not meant to be based on personal failures and successes. It's meant to be an overflow of God's gracious love.

What makes your spouse feel loved? What makes them feel respected?

KINGDOM LIVING

He died for all, so that those who live would no longer live for themselves, but for Him who died and rose on their behalf.

2 CORINTHIANS 5:15 NASB

Being a Christian is more than a cultural identifier or a moral indicator. It's more than a political adherence or an inherited tradition. Christ died for everyone, and salvation is a gift of grace to all who accept it and submit to Jesus Christ as Lord. We live for his glory rather than our own.

May this come to mind when you struggle to love each other. May you be reminded of Christ's sacrifice when conflicts rise up and you find it difficult to forgive. Instead of insisting on your own way remember that you are empowered by the love of God to lay your life down for one another. Your mutual sacrifice is honoring to him.

Think of a practical way to submit to each other's preferences today.

PEOPLE OF GOD

You, O man of God, flee these things and pursue righteousness, godliness, faith, love, patience, gentleness.

1 Timothy 6:11 NKJV

Being a man or a woman of God is a difficult concept to grapple with. Many Christians do not grapple with it nearly enough. We put up caricatures of what manhood or womanhood should look like, but most of what we see and hear is influenced by romantic ideals more than biblical truth.

Don't give in to cultural definitions of manhood or womanhood. You are not expected to fall in line with what the world demands of you. Strength is not an inherently masculine quality just like gentleness is not limited to women. Both of you are called to reflect Christ through righteousness, godliness, faith, love, patience, and gentleness. God's standards matter most, and he will equip you to fulfill them.

Can you see an area of your life where you have placed the world's standards above God's?

THEIR INTERESTS

Do not merely look out for your own personal interests, but also for the interests of others.

PHILIPPIANS 2:4 NASB

As followers of Christ, we are called to display selfless love. This is particularly important within our marriages. Our behavior at home is a window into our hearts. Loving our spouses is our first and greatest ministry opportunity. If our marriage is meant to reflect Jesus, we must be willing to lay our lives down for each other.

It is human nature to be self-serving, but God's grace equips you to grow beyond your human abilities. He helps you become more like him as you follow his example. Look to him and aspire to love each other in the same way he loves you.

How can you put your spouse's interests ahead of your own this week?

MARRIAGE FOUNDATION

Let all that I am wait quietly before God,
for my hope is in him.

PSALM 62:5 NLT

We cannot build our homes, jobs, or marriages on shifting sands. Our hope is only secure in the Father and his promises. People will disappoint us, status is not fulfilling, and our earthly homes are only temporary. All that will remain is what is rooted in Christ. Our hope remains intact despite trials when it is firmly found in Jesus.

For thousands of years the Lord has never failed to do exactly what he has said he will do, so you can turn to him for assurance and completely trust the truth in his Word. You don't need to be derailed by problems and disappointments. Together, remember that God alone is your source of hope.

What is your marriage founded upon?

SELF-CONTROL

One who is slow to anger is better than the mighty,
And one who rules his spirit, than one who captures a city.

PROVERBS 16:32 NASB

All humans seek control. When our control is threatened or things go against our will, we might lash out in anger or emotionally break down. We use all our might to convince others why they are wrong, why we are hurt, why we need more respect, or why our circumstances are unfair.

It's important to take ownership over your behavior. Proverbs reminds you that you can control your temperament. You can rely on God even when you feel out of control. You can operate from a place of peace even when nothing is going your way. You get to decide what kind of character you have, how you react, and how you treat each other. Your marriage is the perfect opportunity to embrace humility, growth, and change.

Have you fallen into the trap of being controlled by your emotions? What adjustments can you make?

FREEDOM TO LOVE

You were called to freedom, brothers and sisters; only do not turn your freedom into an opportunity for the flesh, but serve one another through love.

GALATIANS 5:13 NASB

The freedom we have been given through Christ is not intended for sin. We shouldn't willfully sin because we can just ask for forgiveness later. No, this freedom was given to us so we could serve one another. It insults God and his generosity to use this undeserved freedom to indulge in worldly and carnal activities and habits.

As a married couple, you have the most accurate picture of each other. You know each other's greatest failures and successes. Remember that you are on the same team. Don't let shame or embarrassment get in the way of holding each other accountable to the freedom you have in Christ. Graciously point each other toward repentance and experience the goodness that comes from honoring the Lord.

How can you lovingly hold each other accountable and use your freedom in Christ to build each other up rather than slipping into habits that pull you away from him?

STAY CONNECTED

"As the Father has loved me, so have I loved you. Now remain in my love. If you keep my commands, you will remain in my love, just as I have kept my Father's commands and remain in his love."

JOHN 15:9-10 NIV

We remain in God's love by keeping his commands. We honor him by listening to what he says and shaping our lives after Christ's example. As we follow him, we depend on him to love us with a sustaining love. We live in his love every day, and through his love we find our source of love for others. We need to be connected to the source. If we are disconnected, we will wither away and be cut off.

The love you have for each other comes from God. He is the one who enables you to be selfless, thoughtful, and kind. As you are rooted in God's love, you will have grace to love each other even when it is difficult or uncomfortable. God's love allows you to lay your lives down for each other.

How can you stay more connected to God throughout your day? How might this impact your relationship?

THE CHRISTIAN LIFE

We ask God to give you complete knowledge of his will and to give you spiritual wisdom and understanding. Then the way you live will always honor and please the Lord, and your lives will produce every kind of good fruit. All the while, you will grow as you learn to know God better and better.

COLOSSIANS 1:9-10 NLT

God doesn't give us challenges or tests that are impossible to figure out. He promises us that he will be by our side no matter what we face. He equips us to handle the most difficult trials by giving us wisdom, comforting us in chaos, and reminding us that our strength comes from him alone.

Complete knowledge of God's will and spiritual understanding are not out of your reach. Colossians reminds you that those things are in full accordance with the Christian life. In God, you have everything you need. When you face challenges, hit walls, or feel discouraged in different seasons of life, remember that he holds your life in his hands, and you can expect him to help you.

When you face challenges together, how can you remind each other to rely on God's wisdom over your own?

LOVE IN ACTION

Little children, let us not love in word or talk but in deed and in truth.

1 John 3:18 ESV

Christianity is so much more than a moral standard. In fact, Jesus openly confronted those who saw it as such. He rebuked people who treated Christianity like a list of dos and don'ts. We are not meant to structure our lives around particular rules while ignoring the cries of the people around us. We have been called to actively love, and this requires laying down our ideologies in favor of practicality and sacrifice.

Your spouse is your most consistent opportunity to love well. This means that there will be plenty of times when you need to lay aside your preferences and choose theirs. You get to choose if you will say you love them or act like you love them. You have the daily challenge of putting your money where your mouth is, and you have unending grace from God to do it.

In what areas of your marriage can you be more intentional about showing love rather than simply talking about it?

PROCLAIM HIM

You are a chosen generation, a royal priesthood, a holy nation, His own special people, that you may proclaim the praises of Him who called you out of darkness into His marvelous light.

1 PETER 2:9 NKJV

There is an exceptional difference between a believer's marriage and a worldly marriage. While two people can live together and call it marriage, from God's perspective, there are more requirements. A holy union is something special. We are God's special people, and our lives show the world who he is.

A Christian marriage is a calling. It's an opportunity to reflect the relationship between Christ and the church. Christ laid his life down for the church. He didn't hesitate to demonstrate his love, and he didn't hold anything back out of shame, embarrassment, or discomfort. This is how you are called to love each other.

What is one way you can intentionally love your spouse that reflects the sacrificial way Christ loved the church?

STEP UP

He was amazed to see that no one intervened to help the oppressed. So he himself stepped in to save them with his strong arm, and his justice sustained him.

ISAIAH 59:16 NLT

Jesus was no stranger to sinners. In fact, he never missed an opportunity to defend the oppressed and forgive the contrite. He did not heed threats or buckle in the face of danger. It didn't matter if his actions were unpopular or stirred up wrath; he was, and still is, committed to justice.

Has God opened your heart to help the disadvantaged? Are you ready to get your hands dirty to help the poor, lonely, marginalized, or broken? As a couple, you can be a strong and effective team. You can work together, balance out each other's strengths and weaknesses, and intervene on behalf of those who are hurting.

How can you be God's hands and feet today?

ONE DESIRE

One thing I ask from the LORD, this only do I seek:
that I may dwell in the house of the LORD
all the days of my life,
to gaze on the beauty of the LORD
and to seek him in his temple.

PSALM 27:4 NIV

Even our marriages were not meant to satisfy the longing in our hearts for God. We are blessed with a spouse, and they are a gift from God, but not even they can fill the need we have for our Creator. Everything we encounter has the potential to draw our attention either to or away from God.

Be wary of placing your spouse on a pedestal above the Lord. Does their approval or disapproval matter more to you than God? On the contrary, do you expect your spouse to value your opinion above the Holy Spirit's leading in their own life? While you are one, you still individually accountable to cultivating a thriving relationship with your Maker.

Are you helping each other draw closer to God, or are you expecting each other to meet needs only he can fill?

GOD FIGHTS FOR YOU

"The LORD your God is the one who goes with you to fight for you against your enemies to give you victory."

DEUTERONOMY 20:4 NIV

What battles are you facing in life? Even in the midst of bleak and difficult times, we have the assurance that we have already won the war. This world and its troubles are temporary, but God's victory is forever, and we are victors with him. Our outcome was decided on the cross, and nothing can steal that away from us.

When the pressures of life weigh you down, remember that the Lord God Almighty stands beside you. He is present through every failure and success. He is faithful when your hope is waning, and you are struggling to see beyond your present troubles. He fights your battles, and he has already secured your final victory.

How can you remind each other of God's victory when life feels overwhelming?

DILIGENT AND MINDFUL

"Because of the increase of wickedness, the love of most will grow cold, but the one who stands firm to the end will be saved."

MATTHEW 24:12-13 NIV

Marriage is a marathon. When we start, we are full of passion, but without proper care and diligence, our spark dwindles down to embers. Love can easily grow cold if we aren't mindful of it. It takes watchfulness and perseverance to maintain a healthy marriage. It will not happen by accident or without personal sacrifice.

Your marriage is a gift from God. He has blessed you with it, and it's your job to keep it healthy. The good news is neither of you are alone! You have each other's strengths and weaknesses, and you have the consistent guidance of the Holy Spirit. Embrace humility and he will equip you persevere. Take notice of the warning signs of sin and be fierce in your pursuit of repentance.

Are there any seemingly small compromises that have taken root in your marriage?

SHARE THE LOVE

Beloved, if God so loved us,
we also ought to love one another.

1 John 4:11 NASB

God's infinite love is enough to fill our hearts, pour out into our lives, and spill over everyone around us. The basis of love is not feelings or actions; it's experiencing the love of God and witnessing it change us from the inside out.

The love you extend to your spouse is not given because of how great he or she is but because of how great God is. Living in love and harmony with one another is an expression of gratitude toward your Father in heaven. You can worship God by loving your spouse sacrificially. This means loving them even when it's inconvenient, uncomfortable, or difficult.

When you are tempted to choose your own comfort, how can you put the needs of your spouse first?

ALWAYS SUPPORTED

If I should say, "My foot has slipped,"
Your faithfulness, LORD, will support me.

PSALM 94:18 NASB

In this passage, the psalmist is celebrating God's faithfulness. He knows that no matter how much he would like to promise it, he cannot guarantee he will not mess up again. He is bound to fail in some way. God is fully aware of our weaknesses and persistent failures. His faithfulness is unchanging despite our missteps. He is willing to support us when our feet slip.

God's steady love is your highest standard. He does not discard you when you make mistakes. He does not shame you, ignore you, or expose you to his wrath. Though it is a high calling, you have the opportunity to love your spouse in the same way. Your reaction to their failures can show them God's grace or your own flaws.

How can you humbly reflect God's steady love when your spouse makes mistakes?

CAREFUL WORDS

If anyone speaks, they should do so as one who speaks the very words of God. If anyone serves, they should do so with the strength God provides, so that in all things God may be praised through Jesus Christ. To him be the glory and the power for ever and ever.

1 Peter 4:11 NIV

Everything we have has been entrusted to us by God. He is the reason for our wealth and possessions as well as our opportunities and abilities. When we open our mouths to speak, it should be to honor God and not ourselves. All credit and praise are due to him. When others thank us for our help, we ought to remember to thank God.

Similarly, your marriage is a gift from God and should be approached with reverence and gratitude. Don't take your spouses for granted or act as though you somehow deserve the blessings that come from marriage. Your spouse is a child of God who has been entrusted to you. The words you say and your actions toward them should demonstrate God's unending love for them.

Do your words and actions toward your spouse reflect your appreciation toward God?

ONE BODY

The human body has many parts, but the many parts make up one whole body. So it is with the body of Christ.

1 Corinthians 12:12 NLT

To love each other as if we were one body requires a different perspective than the world teaches. In a culture which promotes entitlement, individualism, and pride, Paul counteracts such empty pursuits by challenging believers to consider who we are in Christ. If we have truly separated ourselves from our sinful natures and been grafted into God's family, then other believers are our family members. We are one body, and we need to care for each other as such.

Within a marriage where a husband and wife become one flesh, this is even more imperative. Marriage is meant to be a picture of Christ's love. Put the needs of your spouse before your own, and you will portray the image the way it was intended. Remember that you and your spouse are members of the same body and should be treated with the utmost care.

What can you do to care for the needs of your spouse today?

LIFE AND PEACE

The mind set on the flesh is death, but the mind set on the Spirit is life and peace.

Romans 8:6 NASB

God wants us to be at peace. He wants us to experience the abundant life that Christ died for. A dysfunctional and chaotic home life may be indicative of an area not yet under the kingship of the Lord Jesus. After all, the same Spirit who reconciles us to God also works within us and in our relationships. The peace of God brings stability and calm into our hearts, and this carries into our homes.

If your life and home aren't peaceful, God is on your side. He is ready and able to help you. Surrender the details of your days to him and allow him to show you areas of required growth. He will gently and graciously equip you to make changes. His leadership is kind, and his burden is light.

Are there areas of your home life that are chaotic and in need of peace?

"In your anger do not sin": Do not let the sun go down while you are still angry.

EPHESIANS 4:26 NIV

We can't always help how we feel, but we can help what we do about it. We can choose which feelings to feed and mull over. Regardless of whether our emotions are justified or not, they are how we feel. What can we do when we feel angry? Specifically, what should we do when we feel angry toward our spouses?

This verse does not tell you not to feel angry; it offers two steps on how to handle your anger in a mature, godly way. First, you choose to show self-control by not following up your feelings with acting out. Anger can quickly lead to regrettable decisions if you do not have control of yourself. Second, you should sort out your feelings and not let them fester. Stuffing down your anger is just as detrimental as letting it overflow.

How can you handle anger in your marriage in a way that glorifies God?

BETTER DAYS

God is our refuge and strength,
an ever-present help in trouble.

PSALM 46:1 NIV

Our spouse can offer great solace and comfort, but nothing in this world can compare to the safety and strength offered by the Lord Almighty. When troubling times come, he is nearby, supplying us with the wisdom and guidance we need. All the strength necessary to make it through the most challenging days can be found in our Father. He is our hope for the future, our light in the darkness, and our peace amidst the turmoil of life.

Rather than turning to your own strength to see you through, or another person to affirm your fears, your first move should be to seek the Lord and lean on his promises. Your spouse can offer incredible love and support, but nothing and nobody else can offer the impenetrable refuge that your Father in heaven can.

What is one promise that God has made which brings you great comfort and strength?

STEADY FAITH

You love him even though you have never seen him. Though you do not see him now, you trust him; and you rejoice with a glorious, inexpressible joy. The reward for trusting him will be the salvation of your souls.

1 PETER 1:8-9 NLT

Everyone's faith wavers at some point. Even the most experienced believer walks through seasons of doubt or even despair. None of us are immune to trials, grief, or tribulation. One of the greatest blessings of marriage is that when our faith feels small, our spouse can lift us up. We can take turns encouraging each other to stay steady when we are tempted to give up.

Your devotion to the unseen Savior is precious to God. He knows that sometimes it is hard to trust in something you cannot touch or see. He is delighted by your faith even when you think it's insignificant. Keep your eyes on him together and remind each other of his faithfulness.

How can you support each other when your faith is challenged?

FEBRUARY

God created mankind in his own image,
in the image of God he created them;
male and female he created them.

Genesis 1:27 NIV

GIVE AN ACCOUNT

Each of us will give an account of himself to God.

ROMANS 14:12 ESV

Our spouses will not give an account for us to God. Only we, and God, know what's in our hearts. No matter how close we feel to our partner, in the end we will stand alone. We must surrender to God on a daily basis and exhibit ownership over our own actions and choices.

God calls you to a life of constant sacrifice. He asks you to lay your life down, and he rewards you richly for doing it. He calls you to humility, and he does not leave you empty handed. Surrender is not a burden, but a privilege and a means for freedom. Don't lean on your spouse's faith when you can experience the richness of God for yourself.

How can you take personal responsibility for your faith while encouraging each other to surrender to God's will?

GENTLE REBUKE

Better is open rebuke than hidden love.
Wounds from a friend can be trusted,
but an enemy multiplies kisses.

PROVERBS 27:5-6 NIV

A true friend cares more about you than they do your opinion of them. Sensitive matters must be addressed gently and respectfully, but truth should always be the prevailing word. A fragile friendship may crumble under offense, but when true love exists, it does not have to worry about the relationship being crushed by critique.

Don't let flattery or pride be the language of your marriage. Set clear expectations about how you each want to receive critiques and honor each other in communication. Spend time learning how to speak to each other honestly and openly. This takes practice, and it isn't always comfortable. Be committed to kindness, and don't be discouraged by trial and error. Learning how to rebuke, repair, and build up is a skill that takes diligence and humility from both parties.

How well do you receive criticism from your spouse? How kindly do you offer it?

YOUR BEST

Whatever you do, do your work heartily, as for the Lord and not for people.

COLOSSIANS 3:23 NASB

Today's Scripture emphasizes the need to work with a positive, fully engaged attitude. It encourages us to please God rather than people with our work. We should have this attitude in marriage as well as in life. When your day requires you to love your spouse, serve them, or work to provide for them, may it be done with a heart submissive to the Lord.

It's easy to become accustomed to the mundane. After many weeks, months, and years, it's not hard to take your spouse for granted. You are used to each other, and you might let certain standards slip. Remember that every single day is an opportunity to serve the Lord by loving well. Longevity of marriage is not an excuse for laziness or complacency. Loving each other is a gift and it you can offer it to God as an act of worship.

How can you renew your daily attitude toward loving and serving each other as an act of worship?

GOD-POSITIONING SYSTEM

In all your ways acknowledge Him,
And He will make your paths straight.

PROVERBS 3:6 NASB

There is so much wisdom and backstory to this admonition which King Solomon gave to his son. He had been down the road of self-pursuit before, had all the worldly wealth someone could ever imagine, and he had seen that it was futile without the Lord.

Acknowledging the Lord in everything and seeking his direction will save you from endless amounts of unnecessary trouble. When difficulties come despite your obedience, you are assured that they are working for your betterment. It is better to seek God and remain on the straight path than to follow your own pursuits.

How can you and your spouse seek God's will and acknowledge him together while you are making plans and goals for your life?

RIPPLE EFFECTS

An excellent wife is the crown of her husband, but she who brings shame is like rottenness in his bones.

PROVERBS 12:4 ESV

To be noble means to possess excellent morals and character. Today's verse speaks of the blessing of a noble wife. It also addresses the burden a shameful wife. In simple terms, a wife's character reflects upon her husband in a good way or a bad way. This verse is easily flipped; husbands reflect on their wives too.

The way you live impacts your spouse. Your choices have ripple effects that can either cause damage or cultivate goodness. From the moment you said, "I do", your lives became intertwined. You can no longer live just for yourself or your own aspirations. Remember how your decisions impact the team and seek to honor each other in all you do.

How does your daily behavior impact your spouse, and how can you grow in character together?

WALK IN LOVE

Walk in love, just as Christ also loved you and gave Himself up for us, an offering and a sacrifice to God as a fragrant aroma.

EPHESIANS 5:2 NASB

Paul says to walk in love. He says this is right because Christ loved us and gave himself for us. His love, as brutally and violently displayed as it was on the cross, is a fragrant aroma to God. It is the truest form of love because it is generous and sacrificial. It is a love Jesus walked, lived, and died in. This is the love we are to walk in.

When you look at your spouse, do you see someone you are willing to give yourself up for? Do you see someone you are willing to not just rely on and be relied upon but someone you are willing to lose your very life for? When you look to gain nothing in return, that is love.

How can you practically love each other without expecting anything in return?

SACRIFICIAL LIVING

I have been crucified with Christ; it is no longer I who live, but Christ lives in me; and the life which I now live in the flesh I live by faith in the Son of God, who loved me and gave Himself for me.

GALATIANS 2:20 NKJV

Self-preservation is strong among humans; it is why self-centeredness comes naturally to most people. A healthy marriage doesn't have room for selfishness or personal gain. The habit of self-preservation must be broken if we want to experience unity and intimacy.

Galatians 2:20 tells us that Paul was crucified with Christ so his sinful, self-serving side would perish, and he could be a new creation. This attitude prevails in strong, healthy marriages, and it enables you to serve each other and glorify God.

What is one area where you can each let go of self-centeredness in order to strengthen your unity and serve each other better?

BEING TRANSFORMED

We all, who with unveiled faces contemplate the Lord's glory, are being transformed into his image with ever-increasing glory, which comes from the Lord, who is the Spirit.

2 CORINTHIANS 3:18 NIV

Previously, our sins separated us from God. There had to be an atonement for our sins before we could approach God in all his glory. When Jesus Christ became our atonement, he removed the sin which was blocking us. He made a way for us to approach God because his sacrifice makes us pure.

The more you spend time with God the more like him you naturally become. This process, known as progressive sanctification, is not something you can accomplish on our own through discipline or good works. It is the Spirit of God who instigates this change in us, and it is for his glory.

How have you seen God's transformative work in each other? Encourage each other with your testimonies.

SUFFER AND REJOICE

Rejoice inasmuch as you participate in the sufferings of Christ, so that you may be overjoyed when his glory is revealed.

1 Peter 4:13 NIV

As Christians we are expected to endure suffering. Furthermore, we are called to rejoice in it. This sounds strange and counterintuitive, but Christians have great reason to celebrate and be grateful when persecution happens. We have been invited us into Christ's inheritance—this includes both the rewards and the sufferings.

If you are devoted to Jesus, you will encounter suffering. There will be difficulties in life that are harder than you expected. When trials come, don't let them throw you off course. Stay steady together and remember that God has gone before you, and he will never leave you. Rejoice as he leads you through one step at a time.

Suffering can bring out the worst in people; how can you embrace suffering as a couple and persevere?

TREASURE YOUR SPOUSE

How beautiful is your love, my sister, my bride!
How much sweeter is your love than wine,
And the fragrance of your oils
Than that of all kinds of balsam oils!

SONG OF SOLOMON 4:10 NASB

Marriage is a precious gift. A healthy marriage is a delight and a blessing. God's design for marriage is meant to produce true joy and satisfaction. We are not meant to settle for mediocrity or utility. We are meant to experience sacrificial love and the blessings that come with it.

There will be seasons when it's easy to delight in your spouse, and there will be seasons when it's more difficult. Practice loving each other diligently and you will create a well that doesn't run dry even in seasons of drought. Find great joy in your spouse and treasure the partner God has given you. Refuse to set your gaze upon any other loves, and you will find that devotion and satisfaction only grow.

How can you intentionally delight in each other especially in seasons when it doesn't come easily?

CLOSEST NEIGHBOR

The whole law is fulfilled in one word: "You shall love your neighbor as yourself."

GALATIANS 5:14 ESV

When the Bible refers to our neighbor, we know that it isn't exclusive to the person in the house next to us. Each person we encounter is our neighbor. Our spouses are the closest neighbor we have. Sometimes we develop a sense of familiarity with each other that gets in the way of intentional love.

Loving your spouse as you love yourself fulfills the law. Treating your spouse how you want to be treated is a demonstration of Christ's love. Adjustments should be made if your spouse continually gets the worst version of yourself. Don't fall into the trap of giving them your leftovers at the end of the day. Loving each other well is at the very top of your priority list.

Are you giving your spouse your best or your leftovers? How can you be more intentional about loving them?

NO OFFENSE

Hatred stirs up strife,
But love covers all offenses.

PROVERBS 10:12 NASB

One common trait of healthy marriages is forgiveness. Scripture says that love covers offenses, and marriage provides us with plenty of opportunities to forgive each other's offenses. None of us are perfect, and conflict is inevitable.

God doesn't simply ask you to overlook wrongs. He doesn't ask you to pretend they don't exist or push them under the rug. He asks you to let love surround the weaknesses of your spouse. This means treating them with patience, kindness, and compassion even when they are wrong. This means refusing to harbor contempt and choosing to empower and strengthen each other through forgiveness.

Is there a hurt or frustration you've been holding on to that God is inviting you to release?

Live in harmony with each other. Don't be too proud to enjoy the company of ordinary people. And don't think you know it all!

ROMANS 12:16 NLT

If Christ, who was the fullness of God, was willing to come to earth and submit himself to the company of humans, then we have no excuse for thinking anyone is less important than we are. Jesus arguably had the only superior position, and he still chose kindness, compassion, and sacrifice. If we want to follow his example, we must do the same.

Pride gets in the way of intimacy and growth. If you are too proud to submit yourself to your spouse, your marriage will pay the price. If you are too proud to admit when you are wrong or learn from your mistakes, you won't experience the unity and satisfaction that humility cultivates.

How can you practice Christ-like humility in your marriage especially when pride wants to take the lead?

REMAIN FAITHFUL

Give honor to marriage, and remain faithful to one another in marriage.

HEBREWS 13:4 NLT

We honor God when we honor marriage. He is the author of the marriage covenant, and it brings him joy when we are faithful to it. We reflect his loyal love when we are loyal to each other. We put his character on display when we lay our lives down for each other.

Honoring your marriage vows requires showing up for your spouse. It means being respectful and loving, keeping your promises, and cultivating intimacy. Your relationship needs more than physical intimacy. You both need spiritual and emotional intimacy as well. Be mindful of the health of each of these areas and protect your relationship by making daily choices to build trust.

What are you doing to protect your marriage today?

GOD'S STRENGTH

My flesh and my heart may fail,
but God is the strength of my heart
and my portion forever.

PSALM 73:26 NIV

The way we live betrays what is in our hearts. When we believe that God has put his Spirit in us, we walk with more confidence and less worry. Instead of concerning ourselves with the small portion we've been temporarily given, we eagerly anticipate our forever portion with God our Father. On earth, our bodies will eventually decay, but our eternal lives are hidden with Christ.

Your body may fail you, or your circumstances might change. Your money might dwindle, or a family member might let you down. The things that give you confidence aren't always reliable. The only thing that never changes is God. He will be your strength through every expected and unexpected storm. He will uphold you no matter what comes your way.

When life feels uncertain, how can you remind each other to find your strength in the Lord?

LOVE AND FAITHFULNESS

"Yes, I have loved you with an everlasting love;
Therefore with lovingkindness I have drawn you."

JEREMIAH 31:3 NKJV

God's love for us predates our existence. He thought of each of us with adoration before we breathed our first breath. His love is the foundation for our existence, and it is the reason we are able to love him in return. He is our beginning and end.

It's important to remember that your spouse has been individually drawn to God by his love. He called them with lovingkindness, and he will faithfully keep them close. You have the great honor of walking alongside them, nurturing their faith, and encouraging them, but you are not responsible for their individual relationship with God. Let him draw them with his everlasting love.

How can you encourage your spouse in their faith today?

TRUE RELIGION

Pure and undefiled religion in the sight of our God and Father is this: to visit orphans and widows in their distress, and to keep oneself unstained by the world.

JAMES 1:27 NASB

Over and over Jesus emphasized that he was not impressed by religiosity or ceremonies exalting pious performances. He preached about love. He taught humility. He lived selflessly. Furthermore, he expects his followers to do the same. Assisting those in need is far more precious in the sight of God than legalistically maintaining an image of devout Christianity.

The way you treat people matters more than the practices you uphold. In other words, the way you love your spouse matters more than your habits or ideologies. Your scholarly accolades mean nothing in comparison to your ability to lay your life down for each other. Your impressive accomplishments will fade away, but Christ-like love has eternal value.

How can you prioritize loving each other selflessly over simply going through the motions of a Christian life?

LIVING BY FAITH

By faith Abraham obeyed when he was called to go out to a place that he was to receive as an inheritance. And he went out, not knowing where he was going.

HEBREWS 11:8 ESV

Living by faith is easier said than done. It's easier imagined than lived. It's a grand adventure, but it can also be nerve-wracking and uncomfortable. God is jealous for your heart, so he will always be on a quest to draw you closer to himself and thus further away from any comfort which threatens his place in your heart.

True faith requires trusting God's Word more than the wisdom of the world. Living by faith means believing God's promises are true and expecting them to be fulfilled. Faith obeys even if the path hasn't been made clear just as Abraham obeyed when he left his homeland even though he didn't know where he was going. Like Abraham, you were saved by faith, called out of the world, credited with God's righteousness, and promised an inheritance.

How can you encourage each other to live by faith rather than sight?

NO FEAR

God has not given us a spirit of fear, but of power and of love and of a sound mind.

2 TIMOTHY 1:7 NKJV

We each walk into our closest relationships with various fears. Some of us are afraid of being rejected. Some of us are afraid of being disrespected or undervalued. Some of us are afraid of loss, pain, or suffering. Intimacy often acts like a mirror, showing us our greatest fears and insecurities. We have the opportunity to see each other at our most vulnerable and call each other to higher ground.

Speak today's Scripture over each other. Remind each other who God says you are. Declare his promises over each other and encourage each other to be renewed by the Word. When your fears and weaknesses are revealed, gently and kindly lead each other toward truth.

What are your current fears and how can you practice surrendering them to God?

SERVING GOD

If you suffer for doing good and you endure it, this is commendable before God. To this you were called, because Christ suffered for you, leaving you an example, that you should follow in his steps.

1 PETER 2:20-21 NIV

We all feel taken advantage of at times. None of us have a perfect relationship, and we all experience strain at some point. Maybe you don't feel appreciated properly for all you do. When these feelings creep in, remember that a godly marriage is not about what you can get out of it but what you can give to God through it.

Follow Christ's example as you serve your spouse. Loving each other won't always be easy, and there will be times you want to quit. Jesus is with you as you endure. He will strengthen you and equip you when you ask. He will give you wisdom, and he will teach you what to do in seasons of difficulty.

How can you shift your focus from you are receiving to what you are offering?

INNER BEING

I pray that out of his glorious riches he may strengthen you with power through his Spirit in your inner being, so that Christ may dwell in your hearts through faith.

EPHESIANS 3:16-17 NIV

God does not lack resources. We spend our lives working and earning money to provide for our families and loved ones, but this is not the case with God. He has glorious riches, and from his great wealth, he strengthens us with power through his Spirit. That Spirit resides in our very souls. It is not a superficial coat of paint that changes our appearance but a deep, transformative Spirit who has penetrated and soaked into who we are on an irreversible level.

Your relationship with God is only cemented through faith. You commit to trusting him and believing that he will do what he says. Each day you decide to lean on his strength or your own. The choice is yours alone to make.

In what areas of your life or marriage are you relying on your own strength instead of fully trusting in God's limitless power?

RESPECT AND PURITY

Wives, be subject to your own husbands, so that even if some do not obey the word, they may be won without a word by the conduct of their wives, when they see your respectful and pure conduct.

1 Peter 3:1-2 ESV

Actions speak louder than words, and respect may be more persuasive than a debate. If we can talk someone into something, a smarter person may be able to talk them out of it. Strength of character will always win over words or judgment. A steadfast commitment to the Lord speaks louder than the best argument.

If you are married to an unbeliever, or you have a close friend or family member who has not given their lives to Jesus Christ, the best thing you can do is respect them and keep your actions pure, so your life stands as the testimony.

In what ways can your daily actions reflect Christ to those closest to you especially when words are not enough?

LOVE'S PASSION

Set me as a seal upon your heart,
as a seal upon your arm,
for love is strong as death,
jealousy is fierce as the grave.
Its flashes are flashes of fire,
the very flame of the LORD.

SONG OF SOLOMON 8:6 ESV

God is love. Today's verse says that his jealousy truly is fierce as the grave. His dedication and love for us is more relentless than death. He will never stop loving his children. We can be confident that his devotion for us is steady and secure.

You are called to reflect God's fierce and steady love in your marriage. You have declared loyalty to your spouse, and you have the privilege of spending your life upholding that vow. Let God's love be your guide. His love is passionate and committed. A healthy marriage is rich in both areas.

How does God's fierce love shape the way you love your spouse?

SUPPORTING OTHERS

We who are strong ought to bear with the failings of the weak and not to please ourselves.

ROMANS 15:1 NIV

The Lord did not grant us freedom from the law so we could use it to indulge in our own desires, but so we could proclaim his freedom to those still stuck in captivity. Everyone is on their own walk with the Lord and at varying levels of maturity. It is not for us to judge, but to love them and encourage their faith.

You have a front row seat to your spouse's weaknesses. This doesn't mean that you get to judge, critique, and shame them. You have the unique opportunity to bear their burdens unlike anyone else. You get to love them with Christ-like love more consistently than anyone else in their life. Don't be irritated by or ashamed of your spouse's downfalls. Stand with them and offer your strength.

Are you a safe place for your spouse to share their weaknesses?

CHOOSE LOWLINESS

Pride brings a person low,
but the lowly in spirit gain honor.

PROVERBS 29:23 NIV

Pride was what manifested in Lucifer, the angel of light. The desire to be worshipped led to his fall from heaven. Pride is a preoccupation with serving ourselves and inevitably leads to greed, stubbornness, jealousy, and rebellion. We cannot serve two masters who have separate agendas. If we are infatuated with ourselves and slaves to our own desires, we cannot serve God in the moments is really matters.

Cultivate a humble and submissive spirit and you will find true satisfaction in the presence of the Lord. It seems counterintuitive but the path of self-sacrifice is the only one that leads to abundant life. Each day is filled with opportunities to embrace lowliness and reject pride. It's rarely comfortable or easy, but it's always worth it.

How can you embrace a lowly spirit in your marriage?

LOVE MATTERS MOST

Beloved, let's love one another; for love is from God, and everyone who loves has been born of God and knows God.

1 John 4:7 NASB

We tend to look like our parents because of genetics, and we act like our parents because of their influence in our lives. In the same way we are meant to emulate God. He is our heavenly Father and the example we were created to follow. The more time we spend with him, the more our character will reflect his image.

Growing in love is part of reflecting God's image. You can't follow his ways, trust his promises, and fill your heart with the Word and not embrace a life of love. Love is what distinguishes you from the world. Love is what declares you are a follower of Jesus. If you do not accomplish anything else in your life, be determined to love well. Nothing else matters as much.

Are there goals or accomplishments you have prioritized over love?

WILLING TO LOVE

"Love your enemies, and do good, and lend, expecting nothing in return, and your reward will be great, and you will be sons of the Most High, for he is kind to the ungrateful and the evil."

LUKE 6:35 ESV

We are only capable of loving our enemies because of the power of Christ. He loved us while we were still his enemies, so he knows the kind of strength we need to love those who have wronged us. There are moments when we feel vitriol and hatred instead of the love we know Jesus expects of us. Those moments, big or small, are opportunities to fall on the mercy of God.

Failure is certain when you rely on any human strength to forgive. Only God has the infinite store of love and self-control you require. He is willing to give them to you but only when you ask him and repent of your own pride. In this heart posture, God can equip you to be kind to people who might not deserve it. Your willingness to love even when it's difficult glorifies God.

Is there someone in your life you don't have the strength to love, and have you asked God to help you do it?

ABILITY

We are not saying that we can do this work ourselves. It is God who makes us able to do all that we do.

2 CORINTHIANS 3:5 NCV

When Paul penned these words, it revealed his changed heart. As someone who had previously prided himself on his own merit, he had discovered his complete inability and fallen to his knees before his Creator. He declared his accomplishments as meaningless, and he rejoiced in God's overarching provision.

Your strength and skills are small in comparison to the might of the Lord. It is God who gives you the ability to act righteously, resist temptation, and stay your course. He is the one who upholds and sustains you. He deserves all the credit and all the glory.

How can recognizing God's strength transform the way you support, serve, and grow with your spouse in marriage?

MARCH

Place me like a seal over your heart,
like a seal on your arm.
For love is as strong as death,
its jealousy as enduring as the grave.

Song of Solomon 8:6 NLT

LOVING WHEN IT'S TOUGH

"I say to you, love your enemies and pray for those who persecute you."

MATTHEW 5:44 NASB

The challenging point in this passage is how we are commanded to love when it is the least natural and desirable course of action. Loving our enemies and praying for those who persecute us is not as easy as cursing them and pushing on with the energy of contempt. God does not promise to help us if we build up resentment; he promises to help us build up love.

You can apply this principle to your marriage. When you feel at odds with your spouse, praying for them is the right answer. Choosing tenderness over revenge, reconciliation over conflict, and peace over pride is path God calls you to. Your actions should be motivated by love rather than proving your point or standing your ground.

When one of you is hurt or upset, how can you lean into prayer and love instead of reacting with anger?

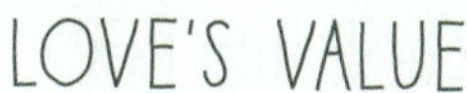

LOVE'S VALUE

If I speak in the tongues of men or of angels, but do not have love, I am only a resounding gong or a clanging cymbal.

1 Corinthians 13:1 NIV

Our lives can be impressive yet carry little meaning. Our list of accomplishments can be long yet unfulfilling. Nothing matters as much as love. It doesn't matter what other people think of us, how successful we become, or how many treasures we gather. Loving the people around us with Christ-like love matters more than anything else.

Loving your spouse is not a matter of checking items off a to-do list. You can do all the seemingly right things and still get it wrong. If everything you are doing is motivated by self-preservation or a desire to look good, some adjustments should be made. Your love for them should be a genuine overflow of God's love for you.

What's one way you can show each other love today that goes beyond words?

OUR HELPER

We can confidently say, "The Lord is my helper; I will not fear; what can man do to me?"

HEBREWS 13:6 ESV

When we are following God, we know that he is working on our behalf. We trust that he is orchestrating our lives for our good and his glory. If we stumble, he will keep our feet steady. If we fall, he will pick us up and heal our wounds. If we get lost, he will lead us back to the right path. There is always hope because God is our helper.

It's comforting to know that you don't have to face life alone. Together you can lean on the Lord and face your days with confidence. As a team you can rely on God's strength over your own. His love is enough to cover your collective weaknesses, and his strength is sufficient for your every need.

When trials arise, how can you remind each other that you're a team backed by a loving and powerful God?

YOU BEFORE ME

Don't be selfish; don't try to impress others. Be humble, thinking of others as better than yourselves.

PHILIPPIANS 2:3 NLT

When we live for the goal of impressing others, there is no room for unity and love. The two different ambitions do not coincide, so we are faced with a decision: us or others. Denying selfishness and choosing to serve other people requires humility. Humility comes from a proper perspective of who we are and who God is.

When you realize how wonderful God truly is, your perspective shifts from self-focus to joyful service. You can live with the big picture in mind rather than being preoccupied with the approval of others. You can worship God by serving others which is far more fulfilling that promoting your own agenda and preferences.

Do you think of your spouse as better than yourself? How can you practice putting them first?

COMMITTED TO THE LORD

"May your hearts be fully committed to the LORD our God, to live by his decrees and obey his commands, as at this time."

1 KINGS 8:61 NIV

Marriage is more than just a commitment to another person; it's a commitment to God. It's a covenant between two people and their Maker. Each love story is part of God's bigger, overarching story. He is the steady foundation of every marriage, and he is the one who holds them together.

Your marriage must be rooted in reverence for God. You cannot depend on your own ability to persevere or do the right thing. Remaining in his love and staying anchored to him will make your footsteps firm even when storms blow. Your connection with God allows you have a healthy connection with your partner.

What does it look like to intentionally prioritize God in your marriage?

GOOD CHARACTER

"Whoever can be trusted with very little can also be trusted with much, and whoever is dishonest with very little will also be dishonest with much. So if you have not been trustworthy in handling worldly wealth, who will trust you with true riches?"

LUKE 16:10-11 NIV

It's tempting to think that a change in circumstances would make all the difference. We think that everything would be better if we just had a different job, a nicer house, or more money in the bank. Instead, God invites us to be faithful with exactly what we have right now. He calls us to honor him by strengthening our character regardless of our circumstances.

Don't fall in the what-if trap. There will always be aspects of your life that don't quite hit the mark. Learn how to cultivate contentment, integrity, and work ethic no matter what season of life you are in. The character you develop matters more than getting exactly what you want.

What is one small area of your life you can develop faithfulness in right now?

MANY ADVISERS

Without counsel plans fail,
but with many advisers they succeed.

PROVERBS 15:22 ESV

Our lives are comprised of a series of choices: what to study, where to work, who to marry, where to live, whether to have children, what to believe, and so forth. Relying on our own insight offers us only one perspective and a limited view.

As a married couple, you have the benefit of a built-in partnership. The perspective you each bring to the table is a gift. It is wise to highly value the opinion of your spouse. Treat each other with dignity and respect and humbly bring outside voices into the conversation when you need more counsel. Willingness to listen to others shows maturity and intelligence.

How can you show your spouse that you value their opinion?

KEEP IT SIMPLE

The one who looks into the perfect law, the law of liberty, and perseveres, being no hearer who forgets but a doer who acts, he will be blessed in his doing.

JAMES 1:25 ESV

The black storm clouds of life and the tumultuous waves of discontent are designed to shipwreck our testimony and set us adrift from the anchor of our soul. James encourages us to keep our eyes on Jesus when we are tempted to become frightened, anxious, or overwhelmed.

As you mature, it's easy to go astray by forgetting what you were taught. The basics of your faith are just as poignant now as they were when you first got to know Jesus. Remember that age doesn't always equal wisdom. Wisdom is found in persevering and steadily walking with Jesus. Continue to follow his ways no matter how simple they seem.

What is one simple truth you can apply to your life or marriage this week?

FREE GIFT

By grace you have been saved through faith. And this is not your own doing; it is the gift of God.

EPHESIANS 2:8 ESV

Salvation is a gift. Furthermore, it is a gift only God can provide. None of us can grant salvation to another person, and we are unable to earn it for ourselves. Forgiveness of sins and eternal life are given by God alone. We extend forgiveness and grace to others because God extended it to us first.

As you experience God's grace and forgiveness, you will be able to offer it to the people around you. If you struggle to be gracious with your spouse, it might be because you've lost sight of what God has done for you. Humbly ask him to soften your heart. He loves to lead his children toward deeper understanding of his mercy and grace.

How can you practically extend grace to your spouse today?

GROWTH MINDSET

If you listen to constructive criticism,
you will be at home among the wise.
If you reject discipline, you only harm yourself;
but if you listen to correction,
you grow in understanding.

PROVERBS 15:31-32 NLT

Many people struggle to receive criticism because it feels demoralizing. We assume that correction equals condemnation. If we want to develop healthy relationships, we must learn how to humbly accept constructive criticism without being defensive. Willingness to learn and adjust shows maturity and wisdom.

Your spouse knows you better than anyone else. Try to hear their perspective even when they don't deliver their critique in a perfect manner. Listening with a quiet heart, asking questions, and being open to change is far more fruitful than arguing or refusing to admit when you're wrong. When humility and flexibility are present in your marriage, you both win.

How can you adjust your perspective from defensiveness to having a growth mindset?

FAITHFUL AUTHOR

Faith is the certainty of things hoped for, a proof of things not seen. For by it the people of old gained approval.

HEBREWS 11:1-2 NASB

The Almighty has a flawless track record of keeping his promises. Our hope in his Word is not wishful thinking. Our hope is assured because God always does what he says he will do. Our faith is certain even though we cannot see the outcome.

Marriage requires faith like any other part of your life. Your faith is not solely in the person you chose, but it is in your Creator. He holds your days in his hands, and he is the one who guides you. He is the one who brought you together, and he will give you wisdom, perseverance, and love to stay together. Your story is still being written, but you can trust the author.

What promise of God are you choosing to believe today even though you can't see it?

HAPPY AND SATISFIED

Enjoy life with the wife whom you love all the days of your futile life which He has given you under the sun, all the days of your futility; for this is your reward in life and in your work which you have labored under the sun.

Ecclesiastes 9:9 NASB

This is a beautiful reminder from the designer of marriage. God loves to see our marriages thrive and flourish. He wants us to be delighted by each other. He intended for us to find satisfaction, joy, and security in our relationship with our spouse.

Worldly advice will tell you to move on to another person if happiness diminishes. The world will encourage you to go wherever your heart leads you. God offers another way. He encourages you to foster the relationship you have. He equips you to cultivate a healthy partnership with the person you made a covenant with. Don't be fooled, satisfaction and happiness are built upon commitment and perseverance.

What do you enjoy most about your spouse? How can you celebrate them today?

RENEWED MINDS

Do not conform to the pattern of this world, but be transformed by the renewing of your mind. Then you will be able to test and approve what God's will is—his good, pleasing and perfect will.

ROMANS 12:2 NIV

The world operates in a particular way, and Christians are expected to operate differently. God's opinion is our highest standard. He is the one who calls the shots, and we live to honor him. His ways are not always the easiest, but they result in true transformation and eternal life.

Let God transform the way you think and operate. As he transforms your perspective, you'll begin to see things the way he does. As you live for his kingdom, your life will become an example of his love and character. Good things come from honoring the Lord.

What mindset or habit might God be inviting you to renew?

TESTS OF FAITH

"The Lord your God led you all the way these forty years in the wilderness, to humble you and test you, to know what was in your heart, whether you would keep His commandments or not."

Deuteronomy 8:2 NKJV

During our time on earth, we encounter hardship and heartbreak. For those who aren't living for eternity, difficulties are just plain difficult. For those of us who hope in the Lord, trials can be tests of faith which make us stronger. They are opportunities to express our love for Christ, act on our commitment to his Word, and be a testimony to those who haven't seen the light of God's love yet.

As you walk through trials and tribulations, remember that your hope is not in vain. Your faith in the Lord is well placed. God doesn't waste pain, and he is capable of using every situation you face for his glory. As you trust his purposes, you will become unmovable in even the fiercest storm.

How has a recent challenge brought you close to each other and to God?

GOOD GIFTS

Every good and perfect gift is from above, coming down from the Father of the heavenly lights, who does not change like shifting shadows.

JAMES 1:17 NIV

Marriage is a good and perfect gift. Of course, it's filled with imperfect moments because it is between two flawed individuals, but marriage itself is perfect because it is an institution God set up to reflect his love for his bride. We get to choose if we will be an accurate depiction of Christ's love or not.

You have a responsibility to show the world how much Jesus loves the church. As you lay your life down for your spouse, other people will see a picture of Christ's love. This means that your love should be selfless, sacrificial, consistent, and compassionate. This is a tall order, but Jesus will faithfully equip you if you ask.

How can you exemplify Christ's love for the church this week?

ALL THINGS

I can do all this through him who gives me strength.

PHILIPPIANS 4:13 NIV

When Paul penned this verse he was talking about finding contentment. He was specifically referencing the ability to be at peace no matter what was going on in his life. We often read Philippians and use it as a motivational tidbit, giving us the strength to apply God's power to whatever situation we want. In reality, Paul is encouraging us to find joy in God even when it seems impossible.

Does your contentment depend on the state of your marriage, the size of your bank account, or the number of items you've checked off your list? Answering this question honestly is a challenge, and it solidifies the importance of what Paul was saying. Being at peace even when life is messy is an incredible challenge. It can be done only by the strength and power of God. This is the miracle you are invited to partake in.

How can you shift your attitude from dissatisfaction to contentment?

BETTER TOGETHER

If one person falls, the other can reach out and help. But someone who falls alone is in real trouble. Likewise, two people lying close together can keep each other warm. But how can one be warm alone?

ECCLESIASTES 4:10-11 NLT

Any predator knows that the easiest target is a lone target. That's why animals often travel in herds and why God created us to be part of a community. We are made to be in fellowship. The give and take of relationships provides us with security, comfort, encouragement, and joy.

Your spouse is a wonderful gift. Walking through life with a companion is a privilege that shouldn't be taken for granted. You are stronger together than you are apart, and you can tackle life as team. Think about all the ways life would be more difficult without your spouse and readily thank them for the joy they bring to you.

How have you and your spouse supported each other this week?

ENTRUSTED TO GOD

Commit your work to the LORD,
and your plans will be established.

PROVERBS 16:3 ESV

If we want our marriages to flourish, we must commit them to God. He promises that if we put our lives in his hands, he will make our paths straight. His Word assures us that he will not let our feet slip, and he will not let us go astray. Success is found by staying close to him and trusting his expert leadership.

Committing your marriage to God requires humility. You won't surrender to him daily if you think your strength is sufficient. You won't ask him to help with big and small problems if you think you already have the answers. You won't surrender the future to him if you think you've accounted for every possible outcome. Open your eyes to your desperate need for God and trust him with your life.

How can you commit your marriage to God in a greater way today?

ETERNAL BLESSING

May the LORD bless you and protect you.
May the LORD smile on you
and be gracious to you.
May the LORD show you his favor
and give you his peace.

NUMBERS 6:24-26 NLT

The Lord's Blessing, also referred to as the Priestly Blessing, was dictated from Yahweh to Moses to give to Aaron for the Israelites. Bestowing blessings was a deeply rooted tradition within the Israelite culture at that time, and this blessing in particular held great importance.

There is richness to be found in taking part of tradition. From the beginning of time God has encouraged his people with beautiful words and hopeful promises. Speaking these words over your marriage and household can be deeply satisfying. Declare God's promises and choose to faithfully believe they will come to pass. Stand together with your spouse as you both eagerly wait for God to show up.

Have you asked the Almighty to bless your marriage? Have you accepted his protection, grace, favor, and peace over you both?

POWER IN WEAKNESS

"My grace is all you need. My power works best in weakness." So now I am glad to boast about my weaknesses, so that the power of Christ can work through me.

2 Corinthians 12:9 NLT

It is hard to appear weak, but the truth is we are all inadequate and lacking. When we recognize and admit our weaknesses, both to God and to each other, we can begin to grow and mature. Our shortcomings are no surprise to God; he is aware of them and still chooses to use us for his glory. God meets us in our fallen state and draws us to himself!

Instead of attempting to be strong on your own, approach the Lord in humility. Put your hope in his power instead of your abilities. He alone can compensate for what you lack. Don't be ashamed of your shortcomings but learn to see them as an opportunity for God to help you grow.

Do you respond to your spouse's weaknesses with contempt or with kindness?

FAITH DEFENDS

In all circumstances take up the shield of faith, with which you can extinguish all the flaming darts of the evil one.

EPHESIANS 6:16 ESV

We can't fight a spiritual enemy by natural means. By faith in Christ's resurrection, we have victory over every spiritual enemy. We can stand strong even when fiery darts come flying our way. We can trust in Christ's promise of renewal no matter how difficult life becomes.

Your faith is your protection. When the enemy tries to tell you lies, you can boldly declare the truth. Your unwavering trust in God and his character will guide you through every battle. Strengthen your faith by reading the Word, engaging with God in worship, and surrendering the details of your days into the hands of your Maker.

How has your faith been tested lately?

Wait for the LORD;
Be strong and let your heart take courage;
Yes, wait for the LORD.

PSALM 27:14 NASB

Strength and courage are found by spending time with the Lord. Peace and assurance are found by trusting him to handle the details we cannot control. We spend so much time and energy trying to hold our lives together when we could be releasing our tight grip and finding joy in surrender.

Look around. Do you see a world of patient, self-controlled people who are content with life and confident in who they are? No, we see a population of discontented, disgruntled individuals who struggle with their self-worth and always seem to be in a frantic hurry. God doesn't want you to live that way. He wants you to experience the contentment that comes from leaning on him. He wants to fill you with courage as you surrender your life to him.

How can you move from frantic to peace filled today?

MOTIVES MATTER

Am I now seeking the approval of man, or of God? Or am I trying to please man? If I were still trying to please man, I would not be a servant of Christ.

GALATIANS 1:10 ESV

Motives matter because God cares about our hearts. If our efforts to please people are simply to garnish favor or approval, that is not an adequate motivation because we have already been approved by the Lord. His opinion is the highest, most qualified one. We serve people because we serve Christ.

It can be easy to fall into the habit of living for your spouse's approval. They see you every day, and you don't want to let them down. Remember that God's opinion matters even more than your spouse's. Honor the Lord, and you will honor your spouse.

Are there areas where you've placed your spouse's opinion above the Lord's?

DAY AND NIGHT

The Lord will send His goodness in the daytime;
And His song will be with me in the night,
A prayer to the God of my life.

Psalm 42:8 NASB

There are times when the sunlight of God's love is blotted out by the clouds of life. Just because we cannot see the sun does not mean it isn't there. Our appreciation and desire for the love of God is designed to deepen through the dark times of our lives. That is why the psalmist's posture is one of hope and resilience. He hopes for the goodness of God and knows that it will come.

How has God given you songs in the night? In other words, how has he encouraged you when life seemed difficult or impossible? Maybe he's reminded you of the truth of his word, maybe he's brought refreshing through an experience in nature, or maybe he's blessed you with the comfort of a thoughtful partner. Thank him for the ways he has led you through the dark.

How has God been faithful to you and your partner? Intentionally recount the ways and praise him.

FIRST IS LAST

"Whoever exalts himself will be humbled, and whoever humbles himself will be exalted."

MATTHEW 23:12 ESV

God's kingdom does not work the way our world works. Here, if you humble yourself at work, the promotion will probably go to someone else. If you humble yourself in an argument, the contender will probably walk all over you. The world exemplifies pride and personal satisfaction while God values humility and a lowly spirit.

With this in mind, which kingdom does your marriage model? Do you insist on your own way, stake your claim, hold your ground, and keep records of rights and wrongs? Or do you put your spouse first, listen and then talk after, and humble yourself for them? God's way is always the best way, and there is always a reward for following the principles of his kingdom.

What are some practical ways you can embrace humility in your marriage?

ENCOURAGING WORDS

Worry weighs a person down;
an encouraging word cheers a person up.

PROVERBS 12:25 NLT

Worry is the enemy of faith. Worry forgets that God is in control both now and forever. Our omnipotent Father is willing and able to protect his children, so we have nothing to worry about. This does not mean that we should turn a blind eye to the realities of this world or pretend that life is carefree and without suffering.

Two things can be true at the same time. Life can be difficult, and we can trust that God is in control. Unexpected difficulties can arise, and we can refuse to worry. Suffering does not diminish God's faithfulness. It's simply an opportunity to rely on him for the strength we cannot muster up on our own. We can't avoid the troubles of life, but we can decide how we will respond to them.

Have you spoken an encouraging word to your spouse lately?

RUN TO GOD

"Fear not, for I am with you;
be not dismayed, for I am your God;
I will strengthen you, I will help you,
I will uphold you with my righteous right hand."

ISAIAH 41:10 ESV

We all have fears, but God, in his righteousness, protects us from sin and death. Evil is everywhere, but we need not dismay at the condition of the world because God upholds us. It doesn't matter what hurdles are standing in our way because God is already preparing a way through them.

God is a just and loving father. You can run to him with every single one of your weaknesses. None of them are too much for him to handle. None of your failures are too grotesque for him to forgive you. He longs to uphold you and restore you. Develop the habit of turning to him despite your sin, and you'll see the fruit of humility, authenticity, and vulnerability in your life.

How can cultivating vulnerability with God have a positive impact on your marriage?

WORDS THAT WOUND

If you bite and devour each other, watch out or you will be destroyed by each other.

GALATIANS 5:15 NIV

Just as living under the law is a waste of the freedom Christ Jesus gave us, living for ourselves is also a waste of our freedom. We have been called to a far greater existence than one which begins and ends with ourselves. Within our marriages, we can daily practice living for someone else. As soon as our intentions and actions become self-focused, blaming and demanding ensue.

Two people living for themselves together will assuredly cross paths when their desires do not align. However, two people committed to serving each other will be blessed beyond measure! Marriage is a powerful yet fragile gift that the Lord trusts you with. Your words can wound, but they can also empower. Decide to build up rather than destroy.

Have you exchanged any regrettable words with your spouse that you would like to make amends for now?

THE LORD'S WILL

Come now, you who say, "Today or tomorrow we will go to such and such a city, spend a year there, buy and sell, and make a profit"; whereas you do not know what will happen tomorrow. For what is your life? It is even a vapor that appears for a little time and then vanishes away. Instead you ought to say, "If the Lord wills, we shall live and do this or that."

JAMES 4:13-15 NKJV

Life throws everyone curveballs: some exciting, some tough, and some devastating. The way we face disappointment can grow our faith faster than almost anything else. We want good things in life, but God wants the best for us. Even when we don't understand, we can know that everything he does is out of his perfect love for us.

Your life may not have turned out exactly how you thought it would. You might have experienced disappointment, unexpected grief, or trauma. The details of your days might not quiet line up with what you hoped for. Remember that only God knows the future, and he knows what is best for you. He is capable of leading you along the right path even if it doesn't look how you expect.

How has God's faithfulness surprised you?

THE SEVENTH VIRTUE

As God's chosen people, holy and dearly loved, clothe yourselves with compassion, kindness, humility, gentleness and patience. Bear with each other and forgive one another if any of you has a grievance against someone. Forgive as the Lord forgave you. And over all these virtues put on love, which binds them all together in perfect unity.

COLOSSIANS 3:12-14 NIV

At the heart of the gospel are six central qualities each of us should possess: compassion, kindness, humility, gentleness, patience, and forgiveness. However, there is one above them all. Love is the highest virtue.

Love is the greatest because it encompasses all other virtues. When you love well, everything else falls into place. Love binds them all together and identifies you as a child of God. You can forgive because God forgave you. You can love because God loves you. This is the gospel message.

How can you grow in love in your marriage?

WATCH

Watch, stand fast in the faith, be brave, be strong.

1 Corinthians 16:13 NKJV

With Christ, we can face our troubles head-on. We can have courage because we know that the God's strength is greater than anything we might face. We can be brave because we know that he will leave us or forsake us. We can wait for him to move because we know that he is faithful to intervene on behalf of his people.

Doesn't life seem like a series of challenges? Once you conquer one, another one is already waiting for you. You can't always change what life throws at you, but you can change how you respond to it. You can stand with confidence, or you can let life's trials wear you down. You get to decide how you react.

How can you embrace waiting on the Lord in your marriage?

APRIL

Love flashes like fire,
the brightest kind of flame.
Many waters cannot quench love,
nor can rivers drown it.

SONG OF SOLOMON 8:6-7 NLT

OUR SAFE PLACE

A gossip betrays a confidence,
but a trustworthy person keeps a secret.

PROVERBS 11:13 NIV

The Lord rewards trustworthy people who know how to respect others. He knows every wicked thing about us, but he handles our sin in a discreet and loving fashion. He is a safe place where we can bring all our troubles. Following God's example, we should strive to be a safe place for others also, especially our spouses who we are supposed to love and respect.

Your spouse's secrets, failures, mistakes, and annoyances are not entertainment for anyone else. Choose to be honorable in the way you handle their private information. Your words matter in both public and private spaces. Don't break their trust by sharing something they wouldn't share themselves.

What are some practical ways you can build trust within your marriage?

DROP IT

Starting a quarrel is like breaching a dam;
so drop the matter before a dispute breaks out.

PROVERBS 17:14 NIV

The book of Proverbs is filled with practical wisdom. It's a treasure trove of sorts for everyday life. This specific proverb is as straightforward as they come. However, the execution is perhaps a little more difficult.

Becoming engaged in an argument is not usually a pleasant experience. Emotions can flare up quickly, and words may be exchanged that cause hurt that is difficult to repair. This is especially true within your marriage. Quarreling often can diminish trust and make life uncomfortable for everyone. With the God's grace you can hold your tongue and use your words to build up rather than tear down.

When you and your spouse break into a dispute, do you consider whether the matter could easily be dropped before engaging?

BECOMING ONE

This explains why a man leaves his father and mother and is joined to his wife, and the two are united into one.

GENESIS 2:24 NLT

When we marry, we take on a responsibility for the bodies of our spouses. We are no longer independent beings who suffer alone, rejoice alone, and make our own way. We are one flesh, and everything we do impacts the other person. Entrusting our bodies to each other requires tenderness and vulnerability.

The Bible frequently compares the bodily dedication in marriage to God's desire for spiritual unification with his church. Marriage doesn't mean living in the same house with someone you like; it means openness and willingness to share your deepest hurts, insecurities, and dreams with someone you trust to listen. It also means being ready to listen when your spouse is vulnerable with you.

How can you honor your spouse's vulnerability?

UNMERITED DEVOTION

This is real love—not that we loved God, but that he loved us and sent his Son as a sacrifice to take away our sins.

1 John 4:10 NLT

Our devotion to God is a response. We are not faced with an unloving God whom we choose to love anyway. We are caught in amazement by a God who loves us while we do not deserve it. The point John is making here is that true love is not a reaction to love received. It is spontaneous, unmerited, and full of grace for another's mistakes and sins.

You can emulate God's love in your marriage by laying down your pride in favor of your spouse. Love them first. Ask for forgiveness first. Put their preferences first. As you each grow in selflessness and generosity, you'll find that your marriage will become a beautiful reflection of the goodness of God's love.

What is one area of life where you can lay down your preferences in favor of your spouse?

LOVE MOTIVE

Love does not delight in evil but rejoices with the truth. It always protects, always trusts, always hopes, always perseveres.

1 Corinthians 13:6-7 NIV

What does real, Christlike love look like in action? These verses offer a beautiful description. Love defends the character of the other person as much as possible within the limits of truth. Love won't lie about weaknesses, but neither will it deliberately expose and shame them in other people. Love believes a person is innocent until proven guilty.

If there is a problem, love takes ownership and doesn't immediately blame the other person. It is not pessimistic, and it anticipates success not failure. Love cheers, encourages, and lifts up. Love does not ignore reality or close its eyes to problems, but it rests on the promises of God.

Which description of love stands out to you and why?

LIKE HONEY

Kind words are like honey—
sweet to the soul and healthy for the body.

PROVERBS 16:24 NLT

A kind word goes a long way. It can have an immediate physical effect on the receiver. When someone shares a kind word with another, defenses lower and the recipient feels calmer and more assured. On the other hand, worry and anger cause actual physical harm to a person's body. It can build up and fester, causing anxiety and illness.

When your spouse thinks about your words what might they say? What kind of impact are you having on their quality of life? Can they look to you with confidence, knowing that your words are like honey, or do they tip toe around your feelings, hoping not to irritate you? It's your job to take responsibility for the impact of your words.

Do your words bring health, light, and sweetness to the life of your spouse?

THE GREATEST

Faith, hope, and love remain, these three; but the greatest of these is love.

1 CORINTHIANS 13:13 NASB

The faith we have in God brings us into eternal relationship with him. The hope we have in Christ and share with those around us has unending value. The way we live by love fulfills the law. None of us can reach the level of humility Christ had, but we must put every effort toward love. Of everything that will last, love is the greatest.

As a married couple, you've likely experienced many different seasons. Faith has anchored you, hope has motivated you, but love has been your greatest strength. The way you lay your lives down for each other is the best indicator that your marriage will last. Love is what will carry you until the end.

What does it look like to love each other well in this season of life?

ALWAYS GOOD

Give thanks to the LORD, for he is good;
his love endures forever.

1 CHRONICLES 16:34 NIV

Gratitude is a habit that must be cultivated. We are not naturally prone to give thanks. It's much easier to complain, grumble, and compare our lives to other people. It takes intentionality to elevate the good over the bad. It takes practice to give more attention to God's blessings than life's trials.

You undoubtedly have many reasons to be grateful. Take some time together to talk about the good things in your life. Deliberately thank God for all he has done and all he is yet to do. Once you get started you'll quickly find that the list is longer than you may have realized. Give God the credit he is due, and your heart will feel lighter and more at ease.

How have you seen God's goodness lately?

NOW AND LATER

"What profit is it to a man if he gains the whole world, and is himself destroyed or lost?"

LUKE 9:25 NKJV

The world shakes its head at us in bewilderment when we exchange what is tangible for what is unseen. It doesn't make sense to trade the riches of this world for the blessings of God and instant gratification for eternal promises. The concept of self-sacrifice doesn't come easily, which is why we need the transformative work of the Holy Spirit.

As God's children, you were created for a different kingdom. Don't lose yourself in the rat race of this world. You can't take anything with you, and it will cost you all your time and effort. Are there things in this world keeping you from giving your all to Christ?

How can you switch your focus from worldly comfort to eternal gain?

COMPLETION

I am sure of this, that he who began a good work in you will bring it to completion at the day of Jesus Christ.

PHILIPPIANS 1:6 ESV

Most of us have unfinished projects laying around the house. We started them with good intentions, but distractions came up, motivation died down, and we failed to finish them. Some of us have relationships we've given up on because, frankly, we lost interest or something more exciting came along.

Unlike us, God always completes what he starts. He never gives up on us, and he never loses interest in us. He has started a work in each of us, and if we continue to follow him, he will absolutely finish this work.

Is there an area of your life in which you've given up hope? How can you turn your attention toward God's faithfulness?

DIVINE LOVE

"Love your enemies, do good to those who hate you, bless those who curse you, pray for those who mistreat you."

LUKE 6:27-28 NIV

Godly love is contrary to our human nature and stubborn humanity. We tend to protect our comfort while he embraces suffering. We elevate our strengths and accomplishments while he elevates humility and lowliness. We steer clear of people we don't like while he welcomes his enemies to his table.

If you want to love people as God loves them, you'll need to experience the transformative work of the Holy Spirit. Trust in Christ's sacrifice, follow the Spirit's leading, and God will expand your heart in love. The more you experience God's miraculous love, the more naturally it will flow from you to others.

How can you and your spouse embrace the idea of loving your enemies?

LOVE CONQUERS ALL

In all these things we are more than conquerors through him who loved us.

ROMANS 8:37 ESV

How loved a person feels can influence their entire disposition. Many behavioral issues stem from feeling unloved and unworthy. Children who grew up in loving homes are more likely to be confident, functioning adults than children who grew up in dysfunctional or abusive homes. When someone feels loved, it can light a fire inside them to do more, be more, and conquer more.

Love is a powerful thing! It can be stronger than guilt, shame, lust, and even self-preservation. God's love is big enough to carry you through every trial life throws at you. It's more than sufficient for everything you need. Together, you and your spouse have unlimited potential victories ahead of you because of God's love.

Are you trusting in the conquering power of God's love or the strength of your own abilities?

TRUTH IN LOVE

Speaking the truth in love, we will grow to become in every respect the mature body of him who is the head, that is, Christ.

EPHESIANS 4:15 NIV

We all love being right. We like proving we are smart, capable, and intelligent. We enjoy the satisfaction that comes from having higher ground. It's vital to remember that no matter how right we think we are love matters more than anything. The tone and delivery of our words is just as important as the content.

A healthy marriage is not built on moments of individual triumph. Keeping track of your verbal victories won't get you anywhere. Kindness, tenderness, and a devotion to love will carry you further than winning arguments. Every piece of truth must be wrapped in the love of Christ.

What are some practical ways to speak the truth in love?

UNIFIED

"Every kingdom divided against itself will be ruined, and every city or household divided against itself will not stand."

MATTHEW 12:25 NIV

When a country is divided against itself, it can result in a civil war. When a household is at odds, it causes disunity, tension, anger frustration, and hurt. Ultimately, it can lead to divorce. If we are of the kingdom of God, and our marriages are dedicated to him, then we should hold fast to godly principles even in the face of conflict.

God is the one who brought you together, and he is the one who sustains you. As you each remain devoted to him, he will keep you unified. As you attempt to stay on the same page with humility and selflessness, he will strengthen your bond. You are an unshakeable team when you both have your eyes firmly fixed on Jesus.

Are there areas of your life where you have let a lack of unity fester and grow?

ACCEPTANCE

Accept one another, then, just as Christ accepted you, in order to bring praise to God.

ROMANS 15:7 NIV

It is God's desire that we learn to live together in peace and harmony. His heart's desire is that we learn to accept each other's differences. This does not mean condoning sin, but it does mean recognizing that our way isn't always the best way. We each have different gifts, perspectives, and minds that work in unique ways.

Praise God for the differences between you and your spouse. You are not meant to have the exact same strengths or weaknesses. Don't look at each other's failures with shame, judgment, or embarrassment. Instead, let your love point each other toward the cross and become stronger together.

How can you grow in areas where you have pointed fingers instead of choosing acceptance?

ABOVE ALL ELSE

"If you love your father or mother more than you love me, you are not worthy of being mine; or if you love your son or daughter more than me, you are not worthy of being mine."

MATTHEW 10:37 NLT

Our love for God is meant to be the overarching definition of our lives. There is nothing that should take its place. It is meant to be our highest priority. When we give God our undying devotion, everything else falls in line appropriately.

Abiding in God's love above all else naturally creates strong marriages and healthy families. With your eyes on Christ, you cannot embrace selfishness, wickedness, or pride. If you are prioritizing his presence and purposes, his love will overflow into the rest of your life.

In what practical ways can you move God up on your priority list?

CONSIDERED CONVERSATIONS

"These commandments that I give you today are to be on your hearts. Impress them on your children. Talk about them when you sit at home and when you walk along the road, when you lie down and when you get up."

DEUTERONOMY 6:6-7 NIV

We live in a world that scoffs at God and criticizes his commandments. They do not respect the Almighty, nor do they obey his voice. Unless we constantly remind ourselves of his life-giving words, other voices will begin to overpower our senses. It is one thing to read the Word of God, and another matter to imprint his words on our hearts so they can be remembered in the moments they are needed.

To take something to heart it must be understood, accepted, and familiarized. As you go about your day, the Word of God should be present. If you learn to lean on them in good times, you will be well prepared for troubles and trials. The Bible is not a resource to turn to when you feel like it or when you have a need; your life is meant to be saturated by it.

What is one way you can become more familiar with Scripture?

APRIL 18

NEARSIGHTED

"How can you think of saying, 'Friend, let me help you get rid of that speck in your eye,' when you can't see past the log in your own eye?"

LUKE 6:42 NLT

As humans, we are so hasty to find fault in others, forgetting quickly to handle our own affairs. Sin truly does blind us, and it is easy to find fault in others while normalizing our own indiscretions. We alleviate ourselves of guilt while heaping it upon the people around us. In truth, this sort of spiritual nearsightedness not only stunts our growth but renders us incapable of compassion and tenderness.

A humble and contrite heart is imperative for growing in godliness. Luke made it clear that we will receive in like measure what we offer to others. If we judge, we will be judged. If we condemn, we will be condemned. However, if we forgive, we will be forgiven. If we give to others, God will give us more than we can imagine!

Have you been overly focused on your spouse's sins rather than addressing your own?

RECEIVED

"Anyone who receives you receives me, and anyone who receives me receives the Father who sent me."

MATTHEW 10:40 NLT

As the time was nearing for Jesus to return to heaven, he began teaching the disciples less allegorically and more literally. He commissioned them to go out in pairs of two and preach his message of good news and salvation. The instructions he gave were intentional and specific.

Anyone who was humble enough to hear the good news and receive it into their hearts would receive God's love and forgiveness. That was the commission Jesus gave the disciples to carry into the world after his death and resurrection. The same commission applies to you. Humbly receive Christ's invitation and seek to model every part of your life after it.

Is your heart humble and open to hear Christ's invitation to salvation and his commission on your life?

WHOEVER LOVES GOD

This commandment we have from him: whoever loves God must also love his brother.

1 John 4:21 ESV

What is the evidence of our love of God? What measurement do we have? Christians sing and talk all the time about their love of God and how he enraptures and completes them. The commandment here is a conviction to show how much we love our Lord not by way of mouth service but by brotherly service.

If you love God, you will want to obey his commandments. His commandments are not burdensome or impossible to follow. He equips you to do every single thing he's asked of you. If you have grown weary in obedience, give your burdens to your kind Father. Experience his abundant love and then share it with those around you.

How can you show brotherly love to your spouse?

EVERYTHING INTENTIONALLY

Above all else, guard your heart,
for everything you do flows from it.

PROVERBS 4:23 NIV

It's important to be mindful of what we allow into our lives and marriages. Our external influences impact our thoughts, and our thoughts dictate our actions. It's foolish to think that we are above being impacted by the things we hear, see, and absorb. We show wisdom and maturity when we treat our hearts with intentionality.

If you have noticed character traits you are dissatisfied with, take a look at your habits and influences. Are your thoughts primarily filled with worldly pleasures and selfish gain? Are you proud of the content you are listening to and looking at? If the answer is no, humbly take steps to adjust your habits. Lean on the Lord and guard your heart.

Are there any habits in your life where you can make adjustments?

WITHOUT COMPLAINT

Do all things without complaining and disputing.

PHILIPPIANS 2:14 NKJV

Grumbling reveals room for growth. Mature adults talk out their problems for the sake of finding solutions not to fill the air with negativity. The temptation to be heard and pitied may result in complaining which is not edifying to the hearer, the complainer, or God.

It's good to process experiences with your spouse, but it's not healthy to be in a habit of constant complaint. Think about how continual grumbling might impact each other. Instead of putting that weight on your spouse, bring your burdens to God and find real relief. Neither of you can truly solve each other's problems, but God can.

As a couple, how can you move away from the tendency to complain?

ROOTED IN CHRIST

As you received Christ Jesus the Lord, so walk in him, rooted and built up in him and established in the faith, just as you were taught, abounding in thanksgiving.

COLOSSIANS 2:6-7 ESV

We are called to walk worthy of our Lord and to be fruitful in our Christian life. This is only possible when we abide in him, trust our lives to his safekeeping, and walk in purity and truth. When we willingly choose to submit to the guidance of the Holy Spirit, we can walk worthy of our Lord.

As a believer, you have trusted Christ for salvation, but do you also trust him with your day-to-day happenings? You have given your life to him, but do you give him your moments and decisions? Do you trust him with your money, marriage, and health? Remember that he wants each of your days and all they contain to be established in faith.

Are you and your spouse inviting the Holy Spirit into your daily decisions?

WATCH AND CARRY

If anyone is caught in any transgression, you who are spiritual should restore him in a spirit of gentleness. Keep watch on yourself, lest you too be tempted. Bear one another's burdens, and so fulfill the law of Christ.

GALATIANS 6:1-3 ESV

Christian love helps carry others' burdens and can eliminate a multitude of potential sins. Christian love seeks to encourage others toward godly living and spiritual growth. We have been equipped to restore each other in a spirit of gentleness and love by the leading of the Holy Spirit.

Someone who is truly mature does not drag their spouse down with judgmental accusations. Instead, they offer encouragement and edification with the hope of helping restore them to their stronger standing. As you bear your spouse's burdens, you get the blessing of having a front row seat to God's miraculous work in their lives. You are a team, and individual victories are team victories.

How can you actively support your spouse this week without judgment or criticism?

WITHIN YOU

Guard the good deposit that was entrusted to you—guard it with the help of the Holy Spirit who lives in us.

2 TIMOTHY 1:14 NIV

The good deposit that today's verse mentions is the truth of the gospel. It's the good news of salvation found through Jesus' death and resurrection. Paul is encouraging Timothy to guard the gift of the gospel with the help of the Holy Spirit. This tells us that we cannot do it alone, and we don't need to depend on our own strength.

The Holy Spirit is your ever-present helper. He makes his home within you, and he reminds you of the truth. You need his help to remain faithful to God. Without him you will depend on your own limited understanding. He teaches you when you are wrong, encourages you when you are down, and prays for you when you are weak. He protects the gift of Christ in your life.

How has the Holy Spirit helped you within your marriage?

CREATOR AND JUDGE

Who are you, O man, to answer back to God? Will what is molded say to its molder, "Why have you made me like this?"

ROMANS 9:20 ESV

We do not hold God accountable for his actions because all wisdom, love, and power are his. He does not owe us an explanation for anything under the sun. In fact, he does not owe us love, grace, compassion, or freedom either, yet he gives them abundantly out of his mercy and kindness.

You can show reverence for God by accepting his ways even when you don't understand them. There will be many times in life when you don't get the answers you want. In those times your faith will either be strengthened or discarded. If your devotion to him depends on your understanding, it will not last. Focus on his goodness, mercy, and grace rather than being derailed by unanswered questions.

How can you and your spouse encourage each other's faith in seasons of questioning and uncertainty?

GOD'S LOVE

I pray that you, being rooted and established in love, may have power, together with all the Lord's holy people, to grasp how wide and long and high and deep is the love of Christ, and to know this love that surpasses knowledge—that you may be filled to the measure of all the fullness of God.

EPHESIANS 3:17-19 NIV

God's love is not based on whims, feelings, or passing fancies. His love is absolute regardless of the cost or of our behavior toward him. God's love never fails, never ends, and far surpasses any worldly love or knowledge we could find. Sin may incur his wrath, but like any good parent, it does not diminish his love.

We are all born with a need to be loved. We long to find someone who accepts us completely and who is worthy of our trust. Family, friendships, and romantic relationships are important, but they can't replace the love of our Creator. What we are truly looking for comes only from our heavenly Father.

In what ways does prioritizing God's love impact the health of your marriage?

AWE AND WONDER

As you do not know the path of the wind, or how the body is formed in a mother's womb, so you cannot understand the work of God, the Maker of all things.

ECCLESIASTES 11:5 NIV

The only thing certain in this world is that things are uncertain. We can predict the weather, but only God knows the path of the wind. Plans can be formed, but they can change in an instant. All things are in God's hands. If we plan our lives according to our own desires and intents, we will face many disappointments and frustrations.

There is great freedom found in letting go of control you don't even have. Open your hands and set your eyes upon the one who holds the sun and stars. Remember that you are at his mercy, and his goodness cannot be matched. He holds each of your days, and he is worthy of your devotion. Stand in awe of him and let your smallness draw you to worship.

In what areas of your life can you and your spouse surrender control?

DEVOTION TO GOD

"No one can serve two masters, for either he will hate the one and love the other, or he will be devoted to the one and despise the other. You cannot serve God and money."

MATTHEW 6:24 ESV

Devotion to God is paramount to our well-being. The world's systems often contradict God's ways, so devotion to both God and the world is not possible. There will come times when we need to choose between the easier path and the right one.

You cannot serve God and money. You cannot use all your time and energy for amassing wealth and serve God whole heartedly. If becoming rich by worldly standards is your highest priority, it might be time for a change of heart. Humbly offer your wealth, or lack of wealth, to your Maker and trust that he knows what to do with it.

How can you honor God with your finances as a team?

RENEWED STRENGTH

Those who wait on the LORD
Shall renew their strength;
They shall mount up with wings like eagles,
They shall run and not be weary,
They shall walk and not faint.

ISAIAH 40:31 NKJV

Hope is like fuel for the believer. We can rise above the challenges of this life because we believe that it will all be worth it. Christ's sacrifice empowers us, and the promise of his return motivates us to persevere. The Holy Spirit walks with us and renews us when we feel weary. He allows us to patiently wait upon the Lord instead of taking matters into our own hands.

Are you tired today? Do you have problems you can't solve? Pray and wait patiently. Waiting does not mean giving up or doing nothing. Waiting is an act of faith because it takes humility to admit you cannot do the work yourself. It takes courage to give up control and trust the Lord.

How can you and your spouse encourage each other to wait on the Lord when life feels heavy or unknown?

MAY

If a man tried to buy love
with all his wealth,
his offer would be utterly scorned.

Song of Solomon 8:7 NLT

Submit to God. Resist the devil and he will flee from you.

JAMES 4:7 NKJV

We have a cunning enemy who wants nothing more than to destroy us because we reflect the Father. He is left powerless when confronted with our almighty God. When we are submitted to God, the devil has no choice but to run away.

Notice how today's Scripture says to resist. Resistance is up to you. It's a choice you make each day. Passivity won't result in the enemy fleeing from you. Deliberately choose God's ways and your path will be clear.

What intentional choices can you make today to resist the enemy's influence? How does this impact your marriage?

RESOLUTE

"If you want to be my disciple, you must, by comparison, hate everyone else—your father and mother, wife and children, brothers and sisters—yes, even your own life. Otherwise, you cannot be my disciple."

LUKE 14:26 NLT

Commitment to Jesus is no small thing. It's not something to take lightly or utilize when it's convenient for us. He is meant to be our top priority. Loving him and following his ways cannot be done casually or by accident. He asks us to give him our full attention.

Marriage is a similar commitment. It is meant to represent Christ and the church. You aren't meant to choose someone and then casually hope for the best. Daily selflessness is required. In honor of your covenant, you deliberately choose your spouse above all else. This is a choice that you will make many times for the rest of your life.

How can you honor your commitment and put your spouse first today?

RIGHT LOVE

Do not love the world nor the things in the world. If anyone loves the world, the love of the Father is not in him.

1 JOHN 2:15 NASB

This world is not worthy of our love or adoration. We must be diligent in controlling our gaze and our affections. It is easy to become infatuated with many different things that promise instant gratification. We must remember that the eternal treasures found in God's kingdom are far more valuable.

You will learn to love whatever you invest in. In other words, pay attention to where your time, energy, and money go. Those things reveal your heart and tell a story about where your affections lie. As you offer your heart to the Lord, he will give you discernment. He will give you grace to focus on the right things.

What do your investments reveal about your heart?

OVERFLOWING LOVE

May the Lord make your love increase and overflow for each other and for everyone else, just as ours does for you.

1 Thessalonians 3:12 NIV

We all go through seasons of finding it difficult to love the people around us. How we respond to our frustrations matters more than the frustrations themselves. God is in the business of changing hearts, and he can increase the love we have for people. He can transform our outlook and help us adjust our attitudes.

If you are lacking in love, surrender to the one who is the embodiment of love. Love is not meant to be a feeling or a casual task. It is a commitment that requires action and intention. Ask God to expand your ability to love your spouse or family selflessly. Humbly ask him for help and he will not let you down. God loves teaching his children how to love.

How can you persevere in love rather than being led by your feelings?

GOD ENTHRONED

In God, whose word I praise,
In God I have put my trust;
I shall not be afraid.
What can mere mortals do to me?

PSALM 56:4 NASB

There is nothing we need to be afraid of because God is on the throne. The most hideous acts and evil plots cannot stand against the Almighty or his anointed. We can place our trust in him with confidence. We can cling to his promises and praise him for all he's done and is yet to do.

Trust comes from proved faithfulness. In other words, the more you know about God, the more you will put your trust in him. If you are not spending time with him, you will be more apt to believe the enemy's lies and fear his empty threats. Hide God's Word in your heart and let your roots grow deep into his love. When the world around you is in chaos, you will have a storehouse of trust built up.

How can you cultivate an atmosphere of trust in your home?

CAUSE AND EFFECT

A glad heart makes a cheerful face,
but by sorrow of heart the spirit is crushed.

PROVERBS 15:13 ESV

Even when tragedy hits and we are grieving, we can still cling to joy because of the hope and love Jesus has filled us with. He gives us peace that goes beyond human understanding and is stronger than any situation we may experience. When we have this joy in our hearts, it radiates through our being.

The condition of your heart can be revealed by your demeanor. Are you constantly stressed, overwhelmed, or disappointed? If the answer is yes, let God do a transformative work within you. Offer him your burdens no matter how heavy they are or how long you've been carrying them. He longs for your heart to be light and for you to experience the joy found in his presence.

How can the joy you experience and carry in your heart be a blessing to your spouse as well?

OUR MERCIFUL GOD

The steadfast love of the LORD never ceases; his mercies never come to an end; they are new every morning; great is your faithfulness.

LAMENTATIONS 3:22-23 ESV

We each have shortcomings and limitations, but God has neither. When we begin to grasp just how awesome and faithful our God is to us, we can relax in the knowledge that he will answer our prayers in his way when the time is right.

If God does not answer you the way you expected, don't become discouraged. Take a moment to remember all the ways he has come through for you in the past. His goodness doesn't change. Your situation might shift, but his love is steadfast, and his mercy is fresh every day.

How can you encourage each other to lean on God's steadfast love through disappointment?

STRENGTHS AND WEAKNESSES

Finally, all of you, be like-minded, be sympathetic, love one another, be compassionate and humble.

1 PETER 3:8 NIV

In marriage both parties bring strengths and weaknesses to the relationship. God calls us to work toward unity despite our differences. He knows that we don't have the same thoughts, habits, or tendencies. He wants us to approach those differences with kindness, compassion, and humility.

Be sympathetic toward your spouse. This is often easier said than done. When a weakness is highlighted, it's not your job to critique or shame. Instead, treat each other with kindness and offer strength for each other's shortcomings. Unity is found when you work together toward a common goal rather than against each other.

How do you typically approach your spouse's weaknesses? What adjustments could you make?

SET IN STONE

*You can make many plans,
but the LORD's purpose will prevail.*

PROVERBS 19:21 NLT

We set ourselves up for failure when we don't align our plans with God. His purposes will always prevail, and it's in our best interest to partner with him. By seeking the Lord and understanding his will, we can honor him with each step we take.

Commit your plans to the Lord. Sit down together on a regular basis and deliberately surrender your ways to God together. Ask him for guidance and reverently listen for his instructions. Cultivate an expectation within your home that his purposes matter more than your own. Give him your days, seasons, and years because he is worthy of everything you have.

What plans have you made for your life? Have you asked God to align your mind and your desires with his?

FEARLESS

Even though I walk through
the valley of the shadow of death,
I fear no evil, for You are with me;
Your rod and Your staff, they comfort me.

PSALM 23:4 NASB

Our lives are a testimony to what has power over us: fear or faith. The psalmist is not promising that those who follow God will never feel fear but rather that we have no reason to fear evil because God is with us. That knowledge is a comfort in the midst of the darkest days and even in the face of death.

Living fearlessly is a practice of faith. It is an ongoing decision to place your trust in God, follow his lead, accept his disciplinary rod of correction, and discover his comfort. There is freedom from fear, and it is only found through faith in God.

In what ways have you experienced God as your Good Shepherd?

CHOOSE HUMILITY

The reward for humility and fear of the LORD is riches and honor and life.

PROVERBS 22:4 ESV

Fear of the Lord and humility are necessary for every Christian's life. Pride whispers that we ought to look out for ourselves, but humility allows us to serve others with kindness and respect. Pride causes us to elevate our own achievements, but humility says to lift up the people around us. Humility requires us to put ourselves last, but the good news is that God does not leave us empty handed. Scripture says he rewards us with riches, honor, and life.

Marriage is the perfect opportunity to embrace humility. There are countless situations where you can put yourself last. You can deliberately elevate your spouse while trusting that God will take care of you. You can loosen your grip of control, knowing that God is sovereign, and he will not let you slip.

In what ways can you practically embrace humility today?

DAILY ENGAGEMENT

"Whoever does not bear his own cross and come after me cannot be my disciple."

LUKE 14:27 ESV

Christ dealt with the problem of our salvation in a moment, once and for all, while nailed to the cross. This issue of our sanctification, however, is another matter altogether. Discipleship means that we follow in our Savior's footsteps each day. We are continuously being transformed into his likeness. This is done through service and self-sacrifice.

There are many parallels you can draw between your marriage and your relationship with Christ. Both require you to make a daily commitment, and neither of them have a tangible finish line. Neither relationship allows you to reach a certain level of success and then check out. You must play an active role in your relationships if you want to see them thrive and grow.

If you've been coasting through your marriage or your relationship with Jesus, what changes can you make?

STEADFAST LOVE

The Lord is merciful and gracious,
slow to anger and abounding in steadfast love.

Psalm 103:8 ESV

Scripture has a lot to say about love and how we should act toward others. We receive God's love, and we share it abundantly with the people around us. His love is resolute, and he looks on us with mercy and patience. He perseveres in love, and he doesn't respond to us in anger.

That is your calling in marriage and your other relationships. When you remember to extend the same grace you have received, it no longer matters whether we feel like the other person deserves your love in that specific moment; God always deserves your obedience. Even in your faltering and wandering, the Lord still loves you, cares for your needs, and shows you compassion. Your calling is to do the same for others.

What steps can you take toward being slow to anger and rich in steadfast love?

PURSUE PEACE

Pursue peace with all people, and the holiness without which no one will see the Lord.

HEBREWS 12:14 NASB

Our lives, especially our marriages, are supposed to be a picture of God's love to this lost and hurting world. Even if people believe there is a god, they may not realize the goodness, peacefulness, and holiness of the true God. That is where we come in. How we treat our spouses matters because our union with them is where our character witness begins.

Live at peace with your spouse. You can be right and still be wrong. What you believe may be factual, but your delivery or approach may be selfish and arrogant. God does not ask you to have the right answers all the time; he instructs you to pursue peace and holiness.

Is there an area of your life or home that lacks peace? What adjustments can you make?

FULFILLMENT IN GOD

Look to the LORD and his strength;
seek his face always.

1 CHRONICLES 16:11 NIV

People frequently enter into a relationship with the presupposition that the other person will wholly fulfill them. Our society paints a picture of finding "the one" as being equal to everlasting happiness and contentment. The truth is, we were never meant to obtain satisfaction from anyone other than the Lord.

The best practice to better your relationship with your spouse is to make time to be in God's presence, to seek his will, and to worship him. Setting your expectations correctly will give you the ability to see your spouse rightly. Expecting them to fulfill your every emotional, spiritual, or physical need is unrealistic and unfair. The goal of marriage is to exemplify Jesus and his bride not to find personal satisfaction.

How can you practice finding fulfillment in God alone?

GREATER GLORY

I consider that the sufferings of this present time are not worth comparing with the glory that is to be revealed to us.

ROMANS 8:18 ESV

Hope is our motivation when things are not going well. It sustains us when times are gloomy and dark. Hope keeps us going despite the challenges we might face in our lives or marriages. It's a force that allows us to persevere even when we are at the end of our own strength or ability.

As a believer, you know that the best is yet to come. One day Jesus will come back and make all the wrong things right. His glory will be worth every ounce of suffering you experience. When trials come up remember that they won't last forever, and perfection is on its way.

How can you remind each other the glorious end goal in seasons of suffering?

A CHOICE

Not that I speak from need, for I have learned to be content in whatever circumstances I am.

PHILIPPIANS 4:11 NASB

Contentment, like love, is a choice. It is not a mere feeling that comes and goes depending on life's circumstances, but an attitude of someone who is submitted to God. Choosing to be content demonstrates faith in the Lord that supersedes what happens to us in this life.

Practicing contentment starts with gratitude. Thank God for the many good gifts he has given you. Deliberately praise him for what he is doing in your life. Set your gaze upon his goodness, and you won't be as discouraged by what you think you lack. Choose to pay attention to his faithfulness instead of dwelling on everything that's wrong.

How can you flex the muscle of gratitude today with your spouse?

ETERNAL INHERITANCE

Day by day the LORD takes care of the innocent,
and they will receive an inheritance that lasts forever.
They will not be disgraced in hard times;
even in famine they will have more than enough.

PSALM 37:18-19 NLT

Food only fills us for a moment, but the Lord's sustenance sustains us forever. God promises to uphold the innocent, and if we have accepted Christ's forgiveness, we are deemed innocent. There are evil people in this world who seem to hold all the cards, but their reign is restricted to their short lives on earth.

Look to the Lord, and you will not be disgraced in hard times. He will stand with you as you trust in him. He will provide for you even when you cannot provide for yourself. Remember that his provision might not look like the riches of the world, but it is far better and more valuable.

As a couple, how can you shape your life around God's inheritance rather than worldly treasures?

A GUARD

Set a guard, O Lord, over my mouth;
keep watch over the door of my lips!

Psalm 141:3 ESV

King David knew that he needed the Lord's help to guard his mouth. He had found his way into trouble because of words spoken in haste and passion, so he sought the Lord and requested his help. All of us need help from the Lord to overcome our sinful tendencies and become more like Christ.

Jesus' words were kind, true, and powerful. He knew when to speak and when to be silent. He was intentional when he spoke, and he is happy to help you follow his example. You honor him when you are careful with your words. What you say matters and the impact of your words shouldn't be ignored.

Are you cautious about your words and how they might impact those around you?

LOVE MADE PERFECT

As we live in God, our love grows more perfect. So we will not be afraid on the day of judgment, but we can face him with confidence because we live like Jesus here in this world.

1 JOHN 4:17 NLT

Life and marriage are about more than growing old. We are meant to grow in love. As we devote our lives to the Lord, our love becomes more perfect. The goal is to become more mature as our hearts expand in our capacity to love like Jesus. The longer we walk with God, the deeper and more selfless our love should become. This will inevitably impact our marriages in a profound way.

When you love like Jesus in your marriage, you will reap a plentiful harvest. Embrace patience, humility, and selflessness, and your love will continue to be perfected. As God's love shapes the way you speak, interact, and serve each other, you will be able to face him with confidence, knowing that you did your best to honor him together.

Are you confident that your love for your spouse reflects God's love?

BEYOND SELF

Love one another with brotherly affection. Outdo one another in showing honor.

Romans 12:10 ESV

Selfishness and pride often stem from fear. We are afraid of being forgotten, overlooked, or neglected. At the core of each of us is a strong desire to be loved, noticed, and taken care of. When those things are threatened, we each lash out in different ways. When we are confident that we are loved, we are free to love others extravagantly.

If you are worried about getting what you need, you won't love others well. If you are constantly concerned about yourself, you won't have the ability to see the needs of the people around you. Remember that God is the one who provides for you. He knows exactly what you need, and he will ensure you get it. Instead of worrying about yourself, turn your attention to outdoing one another in showing honor.

How can you outdo your spouse in showing honor today?

DO GOOD

Do not forget to do good and to share, for with such sacrifices God is well pleased.

HEBREWS 13:16 NKJV

God created us for community. Isolation isn't healthy or fruitful for anyone no matter how introverted they claim to be. The difficulty of our need for people is that navigating relationships can be tricky. We are all selfish to some degree, and on our worst days we think only about ourselves. It's our job to practice kindness and generosity even when we don't want to.

Doing good may look different at different times and with different people. For your spouse, the most impact might be found in the small things like doing the dishes, offering heartfelt compliments, giving them a back rub, or praying for them often. Choose kind acts that speak to them and are meaningful in their eyes.

Do you have an idea of what is meaningful to your spouse? Make a list and be intentional about loving them in that way.

Don't be concerned about the outward beauty of fancy hairstyles, expensive jewelry, or beautiful clothes. You should clothe yourselves instead with the beauty that comes from within, the unfading beauty of a gentle and quiet spirit, which is so precious to God.

1 PETER 3:3-4 NLT

Inner beauty requires maintenance in the same way our outward appearance does. The difference is that inner beauty has eternal value while our physical appearance will fade away. It is far more worth it to cultivate character than to be consumed by youthful attractiveness.

Is your spirit quiet? Does that even seem possible to you? The world is so frantic and chaotic that even the idea of inner peace seems foreign and far-fetched. It's not! Through Christ you can have lightness of heart and a spirit that is gentle and at rest. If God says that quietness is precious, he will help you find it. He doesn't ask you to do impossible things.

How can you quiet the noise in your life and pursue gentleness of spirit?

PASSIONATE UNITY

May the God of patience and comfort grant you to be like-minded toward one another, according to Christ Jesus, that you may with one mind and one mouth glorify the God and Father of our Lord Jesus Christ.

ROMANS 15:5-6 NKJV

Unity comes from God's Spirit as we follow Jesus. Unity has a purpose deeper than simply getting along with other believers. It is a representation that we are from the same family: God's family. We want to be united, so our cumulative praise brings glory to God.

Unity is more than an ideal; it's your calling. Unity is a process through which your marriage glorifies Jesus and declares to the surrounding world what it looks like to follow Jesus. God can give you the patience and courage to have fellowship with others. Together you become like-minded in your love for him and in adherence to his Word.

How can you grow in unity with your spouse?

BUILD UP

Each of us should please our neighbors for their good, to build them up.

ROMANS 15:2 NIV

Each of us has shortcomings, and these become apparent in marriage. Our response should not be to antagonize each other but to help each other out. Sometimes that means allowing your spouse to do things their way instead of insisting it be done the way you would do it. After all, love does not insist on its own way.

The whole idea is to seek ways to build each other up. If you are strong for your spouse where they are weak, and they are strong for you where you are weak, you will have a strong marriage. The two of you can then be a source of strength for others and help them where they are weak.

Which of your weaknesses are matched by your spouse's strength and vice versa?

KEEP IT FRESH

Dear brothers and sisters, we urge you in the name of the Lord Jesus to live in a way that pleases God, as we have taught you. You live this way already, and we encourage you to do so even more.

1 THESSALONIANS 4:1 NLT

Why, as we grow older in the Lord, does it get easier to drift into a humdrum spiritual life? Shouldn't we be more eager and on fire after spending so much time with God? Why do we lose that zest to know him? Life becomes methodical, but the freshness of our first love for Christ shouldn't fade. To avoid this, we need to continually stoke the fire.

The same thing can happen in marriage. You can't maintain the euphoria first felt when love was new, but a routine relationship in which romance has faded is not acceptable either. To keep romance alive takes work and effort like it does in your spiritual life. Deliberately stoke the fire of your relationships with God first and then with your spouse.

How can you bring renewal and revitalization to your relationships?

ENTRUSTED

I am not ashamed, for I know whom I have believed, and I am convinced that He is able to protect what I have entrusted to Him until that day.

2 Timothy 1:12 NASB

We often think about what God has entrusted to us, but what have we entrusted to him? Consider the outcome of investing in the kingdom of God. God multiplies everything that is given to him. When we glance his way, he gives us his undivided attention. When we offer him our meager sacrifices, he turns them into unimaginable riches.

You can't out-give God; he is infinitely generous. Just look at what he can do with a mustard seed. What could he do with a life of obedience? Or a marriage on fire for him? Or a family who puts him first? Think of how your life would look if you fully entrusted yourself to him. Everything you place in God's hands will be the most worthwhile investment you ever make.

Is there anything your life or marriage you have been holding back from God?

LOVE'S STRENGTH

Love is patient, love is kind. It does not envy, it does not boast, it is not proud. It does not dishonor others, it is not self-seeking, it is not easily angered, it keeps no record of wrongs.

1 CORINTHIANS 13:4-5 NIV

Often, we think of love in terms of passion, desire, or the will to do something. Love is a two-edged sword, and the passion of love is balanced by its quiet strength. When people might be impatient, angry, or envious, love is the power within them that holds them back.

To choose to love you must lay down your desire for power, control, and authority. Love is selfless and gentle. Love does not insist on its own way, and love does not seek to be elevated. This is why Christ's work within your heart is miraculous. You cannot love like Jesus with your own strength. You must rely on the transformative work of the Lord.

How does the description of love in 1 Corinthians match up with the reality of your marriage?

NO SEPARATION

"The glory that you have given me I have given to them, that they may be one even as we are one, I in them and you in me, that they may become perfectly one, so that the world may know that you sent me and loved them even as you loved me."

John 17:22-23 ESV

The marriage union is God-ordained and should not be taken lightly. When two people join together, they are doing more than simply following their own desires for companionship. They are taking part in portraying the kind of love and union God intends for him and his people to share.

Marriage was designed to point us toward God's love and help us understand him better. The implications of a wedding are widespread, and the union is felt within the whole family and often the community. Marriages matter to God.

How do your actions show reverence for God's intention for marriage?

BONDING TWO TOGETHER

The Lord God caused a deep sleep to fall upon the man, and while he slept took one of his ribs and closed up its place with flesh.

Genesis 2:21 ESV

God created men and women to be together. He knew that together we display the most accurate picture of who he is. He knew that one without the other was incomplete and lacking. When we embrace it rightly, our unity shows the world who God is and how much he loves us.

The oneness found in marriage goes soul deep. Not only are the details of your lives intertwined, but your very being is meshed together. You find your home in each other, and this is exactly what God intended. The two become one and God is well pleased. Godly intimacy cultivated in a healthy marriage is an incredible gift. It takes sacrifice, intention, and intense vulnerability, but it is well worth every ounce of work.

How can your marriage grow in the area of oneness?

WHOLESOME TALK

Let no unwholesome word come out of your mouth, but if there is any good word for edification according to the need of the moment, say that, so that it will give grace to those who hear.

EPHESIANS 4:29 NASB

How we talk has big implications especially in the context of marriage; it's the difference between joy and resentment. Sometimes a word we don't mean to say escapes and damage must be repaired. Sometimes we stay silent when we should speak and that can be just as harmful.

Remember that words can build up or break down a relationship. Speak your words carefully so you do not grieve the Holy Spirit as you talk. Listen closely when your spouse speaks and learn how to communicate in a way they understand. Put in the work and you will be rewarded with unity and peace.

Are there specific areas of communication that you struggle with? What steps can you take toward growth?

JUNE

Above all, put on love,
which is the perfect bond of unity.

Colossians 3:14 CSB

JUNE 1

BETTER THAN LIFE

Because Your lovingkindness is better than life,
My lips shall praise You.

Psalm 63:3 NKJV

Most of us do not describe things as being better than life. To say something is better than life means we would be willing to forfeit our own life in exchange for this valuable thing. This one thing has to be so valuable that we view life without it as worthless. The lovingkindness of God is that valuable. The psalmist would rather forfeit his life knowing God's lovingkindness was upon him than live a life without it.

God's lovingkindness is better than anything else in your life. His presence is where you will find satisfaction that goes soul deep. He alone can offer you freedom, peace, and eternal life. Praise him today for the blessing of his goodness.

In what ways have you experienced the lovingkindness of God?

DEVOTION

"The mountains may be removed
and the hills may shake,
But My favor will not be removed from you,
Nor will My covenant of peace be shaken,"
Says the LORD who has compassion on you.

ISAIAH 54:10 NASB

Devotion is understood as fidelity, loyalty, love, and care for someone. Marriage is the best example we have of devotion, but it still doesn't compare to God's level of devotion toward us. Even if everything else seems uncertain, God's loyalty is assured. He made a covenant with us which he will never break.

When you accepted Jesus as your Lord and Savior, you entered into a covenant of love with God. When you looked your spouse in the eye and said, "I do," you entered into a covenant with them. Even when everything around you is falling apart, the future is uncertain, and dreams are shattered, stay devoted to your spouse. Lean on the Lord and he will give you the strength to be unshakeable in your covenants.

How does leaning into your covenant with the Lord strengthen your covenant with your spouse?

FIRST THINGS FIRST

"Seek first the kingdom of God and His righteousness, and all these things shall be added to you."

MATTHEW 6:33 NKJV

Everything in life has an order to it. It's important, through prayer and supplication to God, to get our priorities right. Things tend to fall into place if we have taken the time to prioritize a carefully considered order.

Matthew 6:33 tells us that we must first seek the kingdom of God. It doesn't get clearer than this. God comes first before our jobs, marriages, and personal goals. The beauty is that if we put God first in all things, the rest will be added. He is faithful to give us what we need.

How have you prioritized God in and above your marriage?

OUT GIVE

Whoever pursues righteousness and kindness will find life, righteousness, and honor.

PROVERBS 21:21 ESV

God is so gracious and kind. He never sets a standard without reassuring us of the reward. He doesn't expect us to follow his rules simply for the sake of obedience. He wisely guides us through life, and he rewards us when we follow his ways. He loves to give us the good gifts that come a life that is devoted to him.

There is sometimes a level of self-sacrifice that comes with pursuing righteousness and kindness. It isn't always the most comfortable or convenient path. For example, treating your spouse with kindness might mean setting aside your own preferences or giving up your time and energy. No matter how much you give, you cannot out give God. He promises that your sacrifices will result in life, righteousness, and honor.

How can you choose kindness and self-sacrifice in your marriage today?

TOP PRIORITIES

Let us therefore make every effort to do what leads to peace and to mutual edification.

ROMANS 14:19 NIV

If peace and mutual edification are the goals, we must be wary of focusing on our own desires. Putting others first is pivotal in the Christian life. We can't follow Jesus and insist on our own comfort all the time. A willingness to lay aside our preferences is a good measure as to how much we are allowing God's love to be at work in our hearts.

If you are honest with yourself, what is your priority in your relationships? Do you want validation, convenience, comfort, or status? None of these things line up a Christ-like attitude. Jesus laid his life down in order to edify others, and he calls his followers to do the same. Considering how other people think and feel will only be to your benefit in the long run.

Are there liberties you could give up for the sake of someone else?

GOD HEARS

"You will call on me and come and pray to me, and I will listen to you."

JEREMIAH 29:12 NIV

Humans are petty creatures. We are constantly looking for ways to one-up each other. One of the most dangerous results of our desire for respect can come in the form of resentment and lack of forgiveness. When someone hurts us, we want them to feel the hurt they caused us. When they come back to us, even on their knees, there is the temptation to turn them away like they turned us away when we did not deserve it.

This pettiness is not fitting for Christians, and it doesn't have a place in a healthy marriage. Just as God turns his ears to his people, you should turn your ears to each other. Practice the skill and discipline of being a good listener. Pay attention to your spouse, learning how to hear both their words and the heart behind them.

Ask your spouse if they feel heard and noticed. What can you do to become a better listener?

HE IS WITH YOU

"Have I not commanded you? Be strong and courageous. Do not be afraid; do not be discouraged, for the LORD your God will be with you wherever you go."

JOSHUA 1:9 NIV

Shortly after Moses died, the Lord spoke to Joshua and instructed him to take up the mantle and lead the people of Israel. They were to cross the Jordan River and claim the Promised Land. Regardless of the dangers or the magnitude of the task, the Lord promised Joshua that he would preserve him. Nobody could come against him and overthrow him, and everywhere he stepped would become his land. What incredible assurances to be made to one person!

God could do his work by himself, yet he chooses to use people to reveal his love. He will move in and through your life to show the world who he is. He will be with you every step of the way, and he will not leave you alone to face the trials of life. He tells you to be strong because he is the one who offers you strength along the way.

How does the Word of God help you become stronger and more courageous when it comes to handling the issues of life?

HOPE

Whatever was written in earlier times was written for our instruction, so that through perseverance and the encouragement of the Scriptures we might have hope.

ROMANS 15:4 NASB

God is timeless, and his Word is as relevant today as it was when it was written. The wisdom of the world changes with the emotional temperature of the culture. One moral may be trendy for a moment, but there will be a new theme next year.

Hope in humanity is futile because humans without God are bound to fail. Biblical hope is certain because the promises of God are sure. God doesn't get caught up in the fashionable merits of the day; his Word has withstood the tests of time, and it will withstand the wiles of this generation as well. Place your hope confidently in God's Word even when the world feels chaotic.

How can you and your spouse remain steady when the world is full of unrest?

BELONGING

"My beloved is mine, and I am his."

SONG OF SOLOMON 2:16 NASB

At the heart of marriage is the concept of belonging to each other. We are not each other's property, but we have the privilege of being responsible for each other. We are woven together and intertwined in every way. A husband and wife belong to each other just as Christ and the church belong to each other. There is a connection, deep trust, and love that binds us together.

A sense of belonging is a wonderful gift. The connection found in marriage offers comfort, healing, and strength. You are meant to be seen and known by each other in a sacred and profound way. As you delight in each other, you honor God's design for marriage.

How can you delight in your marriage in the midst of the mundane details of life?

LIKE JESUS

In your relationships with one another, have the same mindset as Christ Jesus: Who, being in very nature God, did not consider equality with God something to be used to his own advantage; rather, he made himself nothing by taking the very nature of a servant, being made in human likeness.

PHILIPPIANS 2:5-7 NIV

The King of the universe chose to come to the world in the form of a servant. He could have arrived in all his power and demanded that we serve him, but instead he showed us compassion and came to teach us how to serve others. He washed feet, ate with sinners, preached until he was exhausted, healed the sick, and even gave his own life. He taught us how to love and live sacrificially.

The way you love others matters more than anything else. This is how people will know you are a follower of Jesus. Thoughtfulness, attentiveness, and kindness are more important than accomplishments and success. Embracing humility and serving others is how you display the love of Christ.

How can you use what you have been given to serve your spouse and others?

HEAR AND OBEY

"Blessed rather are those who hear the word of God and obey it."

LUKE 11:28 NIV

Jesus was healing the sick, teaching crowds of people, and intellectually schooling the Pharisees when a woman called out to him. She declared that his mother Mary was blessed for having raised him. Jesus responded that it is even more blessed if someone were to hear the Word of God and do what it says. In other words, obedience to the Lord matters more than status or position.

Adhering to God's statutes sets us apart from the narcissism of this world and fixes our eyes on what is eternal. Jesus made it clear that obedience is what he honors. It doesn't matter where you come from, who you know, or what people think of you. What matters most is following God's teaching and being steadily transformed by his love.

When you read the Word of God, do you look for ways to apply its truth to your life?

EXPRESSION OF LOVE

No one has ever seen God. But if we love each other, God lives in us, and his love is brought to full expression in us.

1 John 4:12 NLT

God isn't simply loving; God is love. It originated with him, and he is the perfection of it. Although we've never seen God's face, we get to experience his character when we love others and are loved by them. This is not merely what we feel but what we do for others.

Godly love is the most powerful evidence of being a child of God. How do you exemplify God's love? How do you love your spouse? Become an expert at putting their wants and needs ahead of your own. This can be done in big and small ways.

How can you reflect God's love to your spouse through self-sacrifice?

A GOOD THING

He who finds a wife finds a good thing and obtains favor from the Lord.

Proverbs 18:22 ESV

The Lord calls each of us to different things, but there is no denying the blessing in having a spouse who loves and cares for you. We receive special favor from the Lord when we lay aside ourselves to love someone else, and it's required for a good marriage.

Do you recognize the added blessing your spouse brings to your life? Can you see the way God is at work between the two of you? Marriage is a remarkable way to learn how to put the needs of someone else above your own. God knows that this isn't always an easy task. Remember to ask him for grace to honorably live out your calling.

How can you deliberately express gratitude for your spouse?

SATISFY YOUR SOUL

Let them praise the LORD for his great love
and for the wonderful things he has done for them.
For he satisfies the thirsty
and fills the hungry with good things.

PSALM 107:8-9 NLT

Marriage is like a good meal. It can be a delight, and it adds blessing to our lives, but only God can fill us to the brim with everything our souls yearn for. God alone can extinguish our loneliness and refresh us daily.

Your spouse is a wonderful gift from God, but he or she is not meant to take away your loneliness or satisfy your hunger. Your soul was made for God, and he is the only one who can satisfy your deepest needs.

Where might you have expectations of your spouse that are intended to be met by God?

PATIENTLY ENDURE

My brethren, count it all joy when you fall into various trials, knowing that the testing of your faith produces patience. But let patience have its perfect work, that you may be perfect and complete, lacking nothing.

JAMES 1:2-4 NKJV

Doesn't it sound delightful to lack nothing? The world tells us we need to hustle to achieve all the things we think we need, but the Bible tells us that it's through patience that we will be made complete and lack nothing. Those are two very different approaches. The Bible is not saying we shouldn't work hard, but it is saying we ought not become frantic and lose sight of the one who actually fills our needs.

Marriage is all about the long game. You must be willing to persevere if you want a relationship that lasts. Trials and conflict are not always an indicator of failure. Rather, they are an opportunity to embrace humility and grow in love. A long marriage is made up of a million tiny choices that probably seem insignificant at the time. Patiently endure and you will be rewarded.

How can you shift your perspective of trials from catastrophic to an opportunity for growth?

DIRECTION

Lord, I know that people's lives are not their own;
it is not for them to direct their steps.

Jeremiah 10:23 NIV

We all know what it's like for plans to change. It's doubtful that any of us are exactly where we thought we would be ten years ago. The world teaches a mindset that is self-focused. It wants you to believe that your end motive should be your own happiness. As Christians, we know that's an empty, disappointing motive. We live for a purpose so much bigger than any one of us, and it fills us with a deeper joy when we are walking out in it.

When you got married, your plans certainly changed. Now, you can't live for only yourself. Marriage is a wonderful way to learn how to live with others in mind, be flexible, and trust the Lord for leading and direction.

How have you seen God's faithfulness through the changing of your plans?

BOASTING

"Those who wish to boast should boast in this alone: that they truly know me and understand that I am the Lord who demonstrates unfailing love and who brings justice and righteousness to the earth, and that I delight in these things. I, the Lord, have spoken!"

Jeremiah 9:24 NLT

We can feed our own egos by attempting to amaze others with our talents or accomplishments, or we can boast in the Lord by declaring his unfailing love. He fills the earth with righteousness, and he wants to call us his friends. That is a wonder worth boasting about!

Every good and perfect gift you have is from the Lord. Every delightful experience, built in talent, or unexpected blessing comes from his hands. There is nothing you have that didn't come from him. Give him the credit he is due and experience the freedom that comes from acknowledging his faithfulness and mercy.

Is there an area of your life where you've taken the credit that belongs to the Lord?

ATTACHMENT

"'For this reason a man shall leave his father and mother and be joined to his wife, and the two shall become one flesh'? So then, they are no longer two but one flesh."

MATTHEW 19:5-6 NKJV

Scripture says that a man will leave his father and mother and will cleave to his wife. The two of them become one flesh. In a Christian marriage, the husband's primary attachment should be to his wife. His wife should be the primary emotional attachment in his life. Sometimes family ties can hurt marriage if spouses are not careful. Other attachments should fall lower in importance to the special bond between husband and wife.

Maybe you and your spouse naturally feel like close friends. Maybe spending time with each other is easy and enjoyable. Maybe over the years you've drifted apart, or maybe it's always taken extra effort to find a level of friendship in your marriage. No matter what your experience is, your spouse is meant to be your highest priority. Oneness with them is worth pursuing. It honors the Lord, and it will add vitality to your marriage.

How can you pursue a greater degree of oneness with your spouse?

ETERNAL CONTENTMENT

Make sure that your character is free from the love of money, being content with what you have; for He Himself has said, "I will never desert you, nor will I ever abandon you."

HEBREWS 13:5 NASB

Those who are led around by a love for money will never know contentment in Christ. They will be easily manipulated because money is fickle and easy to lose. Security cannot be found in money; it can only be found in God who faithfully promises to never forsake us. Wealth can give no such assurance. When greed flares up, money can become a stronghold in someone's heart and push aside the love of God.

God is not willing to share his lordship with anyone or anything else because he alone is worthy. Therefore, you cannot submit yourself both to him and to the pursuit of money. God is worthy of the same amount of praise no matter what your bank account looks like. Submit what you have to him and trust him to give you wisdom when you need it most.

How do you and your spouse ensure that your pursuit hasn't shifted away from God and toward making money?

GOD'S KINDNESS

> *Don't you see how wonderfully kind, tolerant, and patient God is with you? Does this mean nothing to you? Can't you see that his kindness is intended to turn you from your sin?*
>
> ROMANS 2:4 NLT

The reason we refuse to indulge in sin and take the narrower path of righteous living is not to earn our salvation. We are saved by God's rich kindness which draws us to repentance. It is his tolerance, not our good deeds, which saved us from our fate. A repentant heart is all he requires, and he is more than happy to patiently lead us the rest of the way.

Don't let shame stand in the way of being honest about your sin. Give your failures to God wholeheartedly and trust him to graciously help you. Cast your burdens upon him, knowing that he alone can heal you. As you develop the habit of honesty and transparency with God, it will have ripple effects in your relationships. Authenticity with your spouse begins with authenticity with your Maker.

Are there areas of your life where you've let shame or pride keep you from experiencing the freedom God has promised you?

JUNE 21

STAND FIRM

My beloved brothers and sisters, be firm, immovable, always excelling in the work of the Lord, knowing that your labor is not in vain in the Lord.

1 Corinthians 15:58 NASB

Those who have given their allegiance to Christ have the glorious assurance that every promise of God will be fulfilled. Our trust in God's Word is steadfast, and our hope in Christ's return is guaranteed. No matter what trials and tribulations we face, we can stand firm in our immovable faith.

This sort of confidence propels you to persevere in the work of the Lord. It allows you to stay committed even when you'd rather give up. When you love someone who doesn't deserve it, serve someone who can never pay you back, or walk away from tempting sin, it matters. Every step of faith will be rewarded in the age to come. Even if we don't see a return for our efforts now, the Lord is using it. One day, it will all come to light.

How can you stay faithful in your marriage when your efforts feel unseen?

DISCIPLINE

Those whom I love I rebuke and discipline. So be earnest and repent.

REVELATION 3:19 NIV

God loves us and wants what is best for us. He is a kind Father who knows what we need to hear, and how we need to hear it. We can trust his correction and rebuke because we know that he is always good. Everything he asks of us is for his glory and our good. We don't have to balk at his suggestions or choose defensiveness.

God's correction is not always easy, but you can assume that it is worthwhile. He doesn't correct you for no reason or simply for the sake of obedience. He sees your path clearly, and he is always equipping you to live accordingly. It is a blessing to follow his ways and trust his voice.

How have you seen the blessing of embracing God's discipline in your life?

HOPEFUL FUTURE

Certainly there is a future,
And your hope will not be cut off.

PROVERBS 23:18 NASB

As naturally selfish creatures, we tend to read the Word with ourselves in mind. We think about our own lives and how they are impacted. This isn't wrong, but it is important to change our perspective sometimes. Reading the Word with other people in mind can soften our hearts and help us see things how God does.

What happens when you read today's Scripture with your spouse in mind? Have you considered the future God has in mind for them? Dwell on this for a few minutes and think about how you might encourage your spouse to move along the path God has chosen for them. You have a greater impact on their life than anyone else. Use your influence to equip and enable them to honor the Lord.

How can you use your words and actions to nurture God's purposes in your spouse's life?

GOOD FRUIT

The fruit of the Spirit is love, joy, peace, patience, kindness, goodness, faithfulness, gentleness, self-control; against such things there is no law.

GALATIANS 5:22-23 NASB

When it comes to marriage it's easy to get lost in the mundane details of life. Before we know it we're more like roommates or business partners than a married couple. We juggle jobs, schedules, kids, and finances, but we don't always take the time to cultivate the things that will last. We will be richly rewarded if we build relationships that are rich in love, joy, peace, patience, kindness, goodness, faithfulness, gentleness, and self-control.

Is your marriage founded those qualities? Are they thriving and present in your daily interactions? Prioritizing the fruit of the Spirit in communication with your spouse will reap an endless harvest. There is no limit to how much you will gain by letting your life overflow with the Spirit's goodness.

Which fruit of the Spirit needs the most intentional nurturing in your marriage, and what steps can you take today to help it grow?

TAKEN SERIOUSLY

Whoever says he is in the light and hates his brother is still in darkness. Whoever loves his brother abides in the light, and in him there is no cause for stumbling.

1 John 2:9-10 ESV

Hatred is a strong feeling, and many of us wouldn't openly admit to hating anyone. We are quick to say that we love people, but do our actions line up with our words? Do we shy away from hateful language in public and in private? Or do we behave in a particular way in front of people only to diminish their character or express our frustration when they aren't around? These little acts of unkindness should be taken seriously.

Deliberately ask God to soften your heart and correct you when needed. Stay connected to him and his love for you will naturally overflow to those around you. Isolate yourself from the presence of the Lord and hatred will grow like a weed. Live in the light and let love flourish.

Are there little pieces of hatred you've given room to grow? Repent and humbly ask God to redirect you.

HUMBLE HARMONY

Never pay back evil with more evil. Do things in such a way that everyone can see you are honorable.

ROMANS 12:17 NLT

We cannot control the decisions of other people, and we cannot always control what happens to us. What we do have power over is our response. Another person's sin does not permit us to retaliate with more sin. We have the option in those moments to either sink to the level of the perpetrator or to become more like Christ.

It is so tempting to pay back evil with evil. Your tendency is probably to protect yourself, and it takes self-control not to lash out when you are threatened. Remember that God is the perfect judge, and he promises justice for all who follow him. Leave your frustrations, disappointments, and offences in his hands. He knows exactly what to do with them. Keep your eyes on the perfection of the Lord and remember that his faithfulness will prevail in the end.

Do you and your spouse get caught in a payback mindset? What steps can you take to make a change?

FIGHTING FEAR

I sought the LORD and He answered me,
And rescued me from all my fears.

PSALM 34:4 NASB

Fear tends to steal our joy and overwhelm us with anxiety and uncertainty. Instead of trying to push through or deny our fear, let's bring it to God. After all, that is where our confidence and certainty come from. God fills us with courage and hope which outshines all the enemy's threats.

When you set your mind on Christ and his kingdom, the concerns of the world grow dimmer. With God on your side, nothing can stand against you. It's not about ignoring your fear or trying to overcome it on your own; it's about directing your thoughts toward God instead of your fear and asking for his help.

What fears do you need to place in God's hands today?

GOOD PAIN

No discipline seems pleasant at the time, but painful. Later on, however, it produces a harvest of righteousness and peace for those who have been trained by it.

HEBREWS 12:11 NIV

We do not like discipline, but loving lessons from our Father are necessary. He knows what is best for us, and he wants us to experience his goodness. His work in our lives is always fruitful even if the journey is uncomfortable. Growth isn't easy, but it is for the best.

The same thing is true in your marriage. The hard work required to cultivate humility, clear communication, and intimacy is not for the faint of heart. Daily sacrifice is required, but there is a deep richness to be found by the person who embraces discipline. You will not have an incredible marriage by accident. Don't be disheartened by the work but be motivated by the promised harvest.

How do you sense the Lord guiding you to embrace discipline in your marriage?

ONE BODY

Husbands also ought to love their own wives as their own bodies. He who loves his own wife loves himself; for no one ever hated his own flesh, but nourishes and cherishes it, just as Christ also does the church, because we are parts of His body.

EPHESIANS 5:28-30 NASB

We all take time to care for our bodies by eating, washing, sleeping, and so on. Our highest priority, spoken or unspoken, is to protect, preserve, and nourish ourselves. We long for comfort, and we do whatever it takes to find it. We care for ourselves without a second thought. It's second nature and completely normal to put our own bodies first.

This is how you are meant to care for your spouse. Your love and sacrifice for them is meant to be so familiar that it's second nature. When you give your time, energy, and desires to them, you are on the cusp of understanding the love Christ shows his bride. You cannot claim to love Jesus yet refuse to love your spouse as if they were your own body. Honor, cherish, and highly value the gift that God has given you.

How can you treat your spouse as though they are your own body today?

MOUTHS OF BABES

He called a small child and had him stand among them. "Truly I tell you," he said, "unless you turn and become like little children, you will never enter the kingdom of heaven."

MATTHEW 18:2-3 CSB

Christ's followers were constantly trying to appear knowledgeable and important in the eyes of each other. However, Jesus reminded them that this wasn't what he wanted. Children are not distinguished, respected leaders of society. Children are obedient, dependent, and innocent of a lot of things. In order to enter the kingdom of heaven, Jesus tells us to revert to when we were dependent, humble, and childlike.

Jesus' definition of greatness doesn't line up with the world. His kingdom is filled with upside down and backward principals. The first is last. The last is first. The humble and meek inherit the earth. Natural human tendencies are flipped around, and lowliness is embraced. If you want to honor the Lord with your life, strive to humbly embrace innocence, faithfulness, and servant-hearted leadership.

What does it mean to be like a little child at this point in your life?

JULY

A man shall leave his father and mother and hold fast to his wife, and they shall become one flesh.

GENESIS 2:24 ESV

BITTER ROOTS

Look after each other so that none of you fails to receive the grace of God. Watch out that no poisonous root of bitterness grows up to trouble you, corrupting many.

HEBREWS 12:15 NLT

Today's Scripture reminds us that we need to look after each other. It's a call to responsibility and accountability. We are meant to stand watch over each other's hearts and be diligent in our willingness to carry each other's burdens. None of us are meant to follow Jesus alone. We are so much stronger together than we are apart.

You and your spouse are a team. Having each other's backs is part of your team dynamic. Learn how to hold each other accountable with love and grace. Remember that if you are following Jesus, you are striving toward the same goal. Don't let defensiveness creep in and keep you from helping each other grow.

What is the most fruitful way to approach your spouse when you see a sin issue?

JULY 2

LIMITED VISION

Now we see things imperfectly, like puzzling reflections in a mirror, but then we will see everything with perfect clarity. All that I know now is partial and incomplete, but then I will know everything completely, just as God now knows me completely.

1 Corinthians 13:12 NLT

None of us are as smart as we think we are. Time and time again, we realize the way we saw things a year ago was not only inaccurate but perhaps caused us to say things that hurt others. It is Christ's desire that we grow in knowledge and maturity and that we do not allow our perceptions of the world to ignite our anger and frustration hastily.

Don't let pride get in the way of your willingness to grow. It's healthy to acknowledge that you do not see everything clearly. There is grace for what you do not know, and there is excitement in realizing that the best is yet to come. A time is coming when you will experience the fullness of God's glory without any hindrance.

Knowing that one day you will see all things perfectly, what are you most excited about?

DO TO OTHERS

"In everything, do to others what you would have them do to you, for this sums up the Law and the Prophets."

MATTHEW 7:12 NIV

The human heart is often hypocritical. We have a double standard when it comes to what we expect to receive and what we are willing to give. It takes mindful and purposeful action to serve others without expectation of being rewarded. We should form a habit of doing things we would like to be done for us.

This is particularly important in marriage. Practice offering your spouse what you desire. Take care of their chores for the day, give them an unprompted shoulder rub, or make their favorite dessert. By doing this, you'll learn how to better take care of your spouse and make a habit of assessing your own behavior before judging theirs.

What is one thing you wish your spouse would do, and how can you offer it to them without expectation?

CALLED TO FORGIVE

"Lord, how many times shall my brother sin against me and I still forgive him? Up to seven times?" Jesus said to him, "I do not say to you, up to seven times, but up to seventy-seven times."

MATTHEW 18:21-22 NASB

The instructions Jesus gave to Peter regarding forgiveness both superseded Jewish tradition and held a deeper association with a well-known Old Testament passage. It was custom among the Jews to offer forgiveness up to three times. Peter, believing he was being more than generous, asked his Rabbi if seven times would suffice.

In essence, Jesus was saying that forgiveness should be limitless, just like God's forgiveness toward mankind. It doesn't matter what you are used to or how many times you want to forgive. You are called to forgive each other without preference or limit. This is the way of Christ, and you will be blessed when you follow it.

Can you show forgiveness to your spouse as many times as needed without seeking reciprocity or reward?

CREATION OF MARRIAGE

There are three things that amaze me—
no, four things that I don't understand:
how an eagle glides through the sky,
how a snake slithers on a rock,
how a ship navigates the ocean,
how a man loves a woman.

PROVERBS 30:18-19 NLT

It's impossible to understand and explain the depths of love and loyalty experienced uniquely in this union, but it is by God's design. There is a reason he calls the church his bride; he wants us to understand the depth of his love for us, and that was a picture he knew we could grasp. Of all God's incredible creations, marriage is a beautiful one to behold.

The pure love shared within a marriage is one of God's most amazing creations. The picture of God's love becomes clearer the more you and your spouse learn to love each other. You begin to grasp Christ's love as you lay your lives down. It's a beautiful mystery that you have the privilege of experiencing.

In what ways can you embody Christ's love in your relationship?

YOUR RACE

Let us also lay aside every weight, and sin which clings so closely, and let us run with endurance the race that is set before us, looking to Jesus, the founder and perfecter of our faith, who for the joy that was set before him endured the cross, despising the shame, and is seated at the right hand of the throne of God.

HEBREWS 12:1-2 ESV

Everyone's journey looks different. The race we each run is varied and unique. This is true about our relationship with God, and it is true about our marriages. Most of us say the same vows, but every marriage looks different. We should keep our eyes on Jesus and run our race well instead of comparing ourselves to others.

Your path with your spouse will inevitably look different from the person next to you. You will have struggles that other people might not understand, and you will have blessings that other people might long for. There is joy to be found in running your own race. Stay in your lane and humbly embrace the life God has given you. Getting caught up in comparison will only cause bitterness to grow in your heart.

How has your race been unique, and which parts are you most thankful for?

HABIT OF PRAYER

Very early in the morning, while it was still dark, Jesus got up, left the house and went off to a solitary place, where he prayed.

MARK 1:35 NIV

When we feel overwhelmed and overworked, it is important to stay connected to God. He is our source of strength and encouragement. Fostering a habit of prayer will help us stay on course. It will keep us aligned with God's will and plan. Prayer is essential for our well-being, and Jesus knew that.

Consistent prayer can have a monumental impact on your marriage. The love you have for your spouse is meant to come from your connection to God. As you abide with him, he fills your heart with his love, and it overflows to those around you. If you want to prioritize your marriage, prioritize setting apart time with the Lord.

Do you have a habit of prayer in your life? If not, what can you do to create one?

GOD'S COUNSEL

"With God are wisdom and might;
he has counsel and understanding."

JOB 12:13 ESV

Life is full of troubles, and we constantly find ourselves needing the advice of others. We show wisdom and maturity when we are willing to listen to perspectives other than our own. Above all else, we must be willing to hear God's perspective. Our humility toward his instructions is paramount to our Christian walk. It's good to look for counsel from trusted sources, but it's best to ask God first.

Before calling in the professionals, even before going to your spouse, do you seek God's counsel? After all, he holds all wisdom. Develop the habit of bringing your burdens to him first. Invite him into every aspect of your life and become familiar with his voice. He has the answer to every problem, and he has an uninhibited vantage point over your life.

When challenges arise, do you instinctively go to God or people first?

UNITED

Make every effort to keep yourselves united in the Spirit, binding yourselves together with peace.

EPHESIANS 4:3 NLT

God wants us to have peace and unity in our relationships. Strife, constant conflict, imbalanced power, and dissatisfaction are not his design. God did not intend for the marriage relationship to be a taxing or burdensome trial. He wants us to experience Christ's love for the church through our marriages.

There are aspects of your marriage in which God might call you to persevere. There are also aspects of your marriage that God is longing to transform. Ask him what his plans are for your relationship. Humbly submit your strengths and weaknesses to him and trust him to lead you according to his will. He will give you strength to persevere certain things, and he will equip you to make changes if you are submissive to his ways.

How can you intentionally seek God's vision for your marriage rather than just surviving?

FAITHFUL TO THE END

"O Lord, you are a great and awesome God! You always fulfill your covenant and keep your promises of unfailing love to those who love you and obey your commands."

Daniel 9:4 NLT

A marriage is a covenant between two people. The covenant is meant for a lifetime, and the vows reflect this commitment. One of the vital ways believers start the marriage journey is by involving God from the very beginning. As the author of the greatest covenant of all time, God will provide a solid foundation as nothing else can. He can help us keep our promises because he has never failed to keep one of his.

When it feels like a joy to stay committed to your spouse, lean on the Lord. When you are tempted to stray in any way, lean on the Lord. Your vows will be tested in various ways throughout your marriage. If you invite him in, God will remain with you through every trial and season of blessing. He will equip you to be faithful to the promises you made.

In what ways are you inviting the Lord to help you uphold your vows?

ENCHANTING LOVE

You have enchanted my heart, my sister, my bride;
You have enchanted my heart
with a single glance of your eyes,
With a single strand of your necklace.

Song of Solomon 4:9 NASB

It's likely we can all remember a time when we were enchanted by our spouse. The age-old tale is one of early days filled with burning passion that fades over the years. It's a common stereotype that newlyweds are enthralled with each other while old married couples bicker and tolerate each other. It can be encouraging to remember that this doesn't have to be the story.

It's always worthwhile to cultivate passion in your marriage. Don't fall for the lie that only the young are enraptured with each other. Strive to cherish your spouse all of your days and ask God to renew your perspective on days that are difficult. Being enchanted by each other doesn't have to be left in the past. Loyal, committed, and faithful love can also be passionate and fiery.

What are some practical ways to cultivate passion in your marriage?

DAILY SAVORING

Every time I think of you, I give thanks to my God.

PHILIPPIANS 1:3 NLT

In this passage, Paul is rejoicing in the faith of the church of Philippi and giving thanks to the Lord who is shaping them to be his people. In the same way, we ought to apply this principle to our own lives and rejoice when the ones we care about so deeply are similarly being used and shaped by God. We rejoice in their growth and in the glory their lives bring to our Savior.

Having someone you love more than life itself is beautiful. Your spouse is meant to be a gift from God to help you both understand him and represent him better. When your heart is aligned with God, you cannot help but thank him for the incredible blessing of the person you love most. If you see them succeed, rejoice on their behalf. When you witness their sorrow, comfort them just as your Father comforts you.

Have you made an effort to thank God for your spouse?

GOD'S PERSPECTIVE

"Do not look on his appearance or on the height of his stature, because I have rejected him. For the LORD sees not as man sees: man looks on the outward appearance, but the LORD looks on the heart."

1 SAMUEL 16:7 ESV

We should focus more of our attention on the condition of our hearts than our physical appearance or our reputation. God looks deeper than skin and considers the motivations of our hearts. He chose David to be king even though David was not impressive in physique or stature.

If you ask him, God will teach you how to see past outward appearances. Strong character is far more important than how someone looks. While it's great to find your spouse physically attractive, it's not the most important part of who they are. As a team, be devoted to developing faithfulness and character over outward attraction which will surely fade away.

How can you align your perspective with God's when it comes to physical appearances?

QUICK TO LISTEN

Let every person be quick to hear, slow to speak, slow to anger; for the anger of man does not produce the righteousness of God.

JAMES 1:19-20 ESV

Relationships need to be carefully and prayerfully protected. We spend the most time with our spouse, so it makes sense that they would be most susceptible to our flaws and frustrations. The hurt we cause with our words can cause deep pain because we are supposed to be a safe and loving refuge for each other. For the sake of our marriages and in response to God's wisdom, let us make sure we are listening, speaking carefully, and choosing righteousness over anger.

It's easy to open our mouths and hastily respond in the flesh rather than pondering our words and replying in godly wisdom. Do you ever bite your tongue too late and wish you could rewind the conversation? Angry words can damage a relationship in seconds. Misunderstandings and jumping to conclusions can cause us to carelessly lash out and wound deeply.

If you ask your spouse, would they say you are slow to anger and quick to listen?

BURDENS

Cast your burden on the LORD,
And He shall sustain you;
He shall never permit the righteous to be moved.

PSALM 55:22 NKJV

Most of us carry unnecessary burdens. We stubbornly insist on managing alone even though God offers us his incredible strength. Some of us do this because we forget God's invitation. Some of us don't think we are worthy of God's help. Some of us aren't convinced of God's goodness. In any case, God's faithfulness is not impacted by our faithlessness. He longs to sustain us and give us the help we need.

What burdens are you carrying today? Are worries in your life causing sleepless nights or anxiety? Are you easily set off by your spouse or having a hard time trusting them? You may be shouldering a load you were never meant to carry. The Lord is always nearby and ready to lift what you cannot. Your Father offers unparalleled rest, peace, strength, and endurance so you can do everything you're supposed to.

What unnecessary burdens have you been shouldering?

WEAK BUT WILLING

He gives strength to the weary and increases the power of the weak.

ISAIAH 40:29 NIV

God sees our weaknesses, and he is not discouraged by them. He wants to give us his power and strength. He is not disappointed in us when we don't have it all together, and he is not surprised by our failures and shortcomings. He is not constantly waiting for us to mess up, and he is not eager to point his finger and create shame. He is infinitely kind, and always ready to comfort us in our weariness.

Rest in him. Offer him your broken gifts, weak faith, and humble willingness. Offer yourself to him in whatever condition you happen to be in today because that's all he is asking of you. Invite him into the reality of your life and trust him to strengthen you where you are weak. You don't need to put up a front or convince him of your worthiness.

How have you seen God meet you in your humility and brokenness?

SET FREE

Stand fast therefore in the liberty by which Christ has made us free, and do not be entangled again with a yoke of bondage.

GALATIANS 5:1 NKJV

It may sound ridiculous, but we are often the authors of our own enslavement. We wallow in guilt, try to earn God's approval through good works, and scurry back to our old sin. We are prone to forgetting the glorious freedom that Jesus purchased for us. We are not enslaved any longer; we are God's children. As such, we need to stand confidently in our freedom and refuse to let the devil place his yoke on us.

If someone bought you a brand-new mansion, would you choose to live in a tent in the backyard instead? Christ paid a high price for your freedom. He is preparing the most amazing home for you, so why would you choose chains? Don't sit in bondage when he has given you the key to your freedom.

Are there areas of life where you or your spouse behave like a slave rather than someone who has been set free?

HE HEARS

We are confident that he hears us whenever we ask for anything that pleases him.

1 John 5:14 NLT

God promises to hear us when our hearts are aligned with his. This is such a wonderful and comforting promise! If we want to have a fruitful prayer life, we must take the time to learn what pleases God. The more we get to know him the more we will understand his good and perfect will. The more we follow his Spirit the more we will see his plans and purposes.

May God's will unfold in your life and marriage. May you be soft hearted toward his instructions and willing to be transformed into his likeness. May you choose his ways above your own, knowing that his path will always lead to eternal life.

How can you shift your prayers from being focused on your will toward being focused on God's will?

GIVE

"Give, and it will be given to you: good measure, pressed down, shaken together, and running over will be put into your bosom. For with the same measure that you use, it will be measured back to you."

Luke 6:38 NKJV

We cannot possibly outgive God. He is proud of us when we are generous because it shows genuine care for each other, and it proves we trust him to supply for our needs. We don't need to worry about what we don't have. He will repay us with his heavenly gifts.

Anyone can give out of their abundance, but when you give out of your need, the Lord is quick to multiply it. It's rarely convenient to be generous, but it is always worth it. You don't have to be wealthy to live a generous lifestyle. You can be an extravagant giver with your words, time, and energy. Every gift you give in the name of love matters.

How can you and your spouse cultivate an atmosphere of generosity in your home?

EACH MORNING

Let me hear Your faithfulness in the morning,
For I trust in You;
Teach me the way in which I should walk;
For to You I lift up my soul.

PSALM 143:8 NASB

Each morning brings a new opportunity to be renewed by God's love. Each day is fresh, and God's mercies are new. He invites us to remember his faithfulness and look to him for guidance. As the sun rises, we can turn eyes to him and acknowledge his lordship over our lives.

You get to set the tone in your home. You can wake up, choose peace, and surrender anew to the Lord, or you can allow your current stress and frustration to rule the day. Let your trust in God filter into how you start your day, and your home will follow. Everyone will enjoy the fruit that comes from honoring him from the very start.

How can you set the tone for your home each morning?

RETURN TO THE LORD

Let the wicked abandon his way,
And the unrighteous person his thoughts;
And let him return to the LORD,
And He will have compassion on him,
And to our God,
For He will abundantly pardon.

ISAIAH 55:7 NASB

Sometimes sin convinces us we are too far gone to return to righteousness. We look at the red on our ledgers, and we convince ourselves there is no hope; we might as well give up. Perhaps we decide that if we have sinned already, we might as well sin all the more since there is no going back.

Don't let your perceived distance from God interfere with his grace. He longs to forgive you and show you mercy. You are never too far gone. There is no path you can wander that will lead you to a place God cannot find you. Call upon his name and he will have compassion on you.

Is there an area of life where you've allowed guilt or shame to keep you from calling out to God?

DOWN THE LINE

Your wife will be like a fruitful grapevine,
flourishing within your home.
Your children will be like vigorous young olive trees
as they sit around your table.

PSALM 128:3 NLT

God's blessings impact more than individuals. When we decide to follow and obey God, many other people are blessed as a result. He graciously intervenes on behalf of his people, and his faithfulness is seen through generations. God is generous, and his blessings multiply. Although our bad actions have consequences that can impact other people, the blessings that accompany our obedience travel much further down the line.

When you make a decision, do you think about how it will affect your spouse for better or worse? Do you consider his or her well-being as well as your own? Remember that your obedience to God will have a positive impact on your household. Likewise, your disobedience or passivity will also shape your home. Honor the Lord for his glory, your good, and the good of those around you.

How have you seen your positive or negative decisions shape your home?

LOVE COVERS

Above all, keep loving one another earnestly, since love covers a multitude of sins.

1 PETER 4:8 ESV

Love does not treat others critically or mercilessly. If we put others down, it means we are also moving downwards. Pulling others up is how we climb. As a society, and especially as a married couple, we rise or fall together. Ridiculing our spouses only hurts the other half of us since we are one.

Loving your spouse does not mean that you dismiss their sin, but it does mean that you forgive them when they are sorry, bear with them as they heal, and humbly remember your own need for forgiveness. Christ's love for you covered your sins and washed you clean. This divine love is not blind to faults, but it is gracious and patient.

What are some practical ways you can cover your spouse's sins with love?

GOD'S VIRTUE

The LORD passed before him and proclaimed, "The LORD, the LORD, a God merciful and gracious, slow to anger, and abounding in steadfast love and faithfulness."

EXODUS 34:6 ESV

God Almighty himself, appearing in a cloud before Moses, could have given himself any accolade he wanted. He could have appeared as mighty, powerful, and important, yet he chose to identify as the Lord of mercy, grace, and love. How dare we squabble and elevate ourselves while God stoops low to be with us?

You will be elevated by embracing lowliness. As you humbly depend on the Lord over your own strength, you will experience the goodness of his presence all the more. There will be many opportunities in marriage to insist on your own way or pridefully declare your superiority. Instead of giving in to your flesh, remember that humility is the way of Jesus.

How can you embrace the virtue of humility today?

LOVE AND ACTION

"Truly I tell you, whatever you did for one of the least of these brothers and sisters of mine, you did for me."

MATTHEW 25:40 NIV

God, in his abounding love, did not sit idle while we were in sin but sent his Son to us. In the same way, God wants us to show our love for those around us by giving food to the hungry, water to the thirsty, and a place of belonging to the estranged. The difficulty is that it can be uncomfortable, and we are often as blind to the needs of our closest people as we are to strangers' needs.

Most people treat strangers more courteously than their own children and spouse, but we need to remember that "the least of these" might just be sharing our bed. Perhaps he or she is the one from whom we are withholding our generosity. We should seek to love each other through our actions rather than just our words.

Does your spouse have needs that you have overlooked?

SOWING AND REAPING

Do not be deceived: God cannot be mocked. A man reaps what he sows. Whoever sows to please their flesh, from the flesh will reap destruction; whoever sows to please the Spirit, from the Spirit will reap eternal life.

GALATIANS 6:7-8 NIV

Although God can supersede any natural law, he fashioned them with a purpose, and he usually allows them to run their course. Basic logic maintains that outcomes match inputs. By that reasoning, what we put into our marriage will directly correlate with what we get out of it.

Do you take your spouse for granted, or do you treat them like the gift from God that they are? You can't withdraw more than you deposit. The crop we harvest has everything to do with the seeds we plant long beforehand. God's natural law of cause and effect applies to marriage the same way it does to anything else. Don't be deceived; the fruit in your marriage comes directly from the work you put into tending it.

Are there areas of marriage where you have been expecting a bountiful harvest for little work?

AUTHORITY OF SCRIPTURE

All Scripture is God-breathed and is useful for teaching, rebuking, correcting and training in righteousness, so that the servant of God may be thoroughly equipped for every good work.

2 Timothy 3:16-17 NIV

It is no surprise that the Word of God is useful for many things necessary in a Christian's life. It unveils God's holy character and teaches us his divine plan for mankind. It convicts us of our need for a savior and helps us understand our involvement in God's plan. It informs us what God expects of his children and guides us along the road of righteous living. It encourages us when we are weary, and it comforts us when we face trials of many kinds.

God's Word is powerful, and it is a critical element for building an unshakeable foundation in your marriage. You might feel awkward reading Scripture together at first, but the discomfort is worth the reward. You will grow together and with the Lord as you value his Word in your home.

In what ways can you incorporate more of the Word in your everyday life?

"Peace I leave with you; my peace I give you. I do not give to you as the world gives. Do not let your hearts be troubled and do not be afraid."

JOHN 14:27 NIV

Jesus spoke these words to his disciples in preparation for what he knew was about to happen. He was going to be arrested and crucified, and his disciples would scatter. They would feel lost and confused until Jesus returned to them and testified of God's miraculous salvation. He encouraged them that his Spirit of peace would remain with them until the end of their days.

God does not leave you unprepared or alone. He always prepares you for what is coming and walks with you every step of the way. He faithfully guides you, and he gives you peace whenever you need it. He fills you with hope, encourages your soul, and equips you for whatever the future will hold.

How have you experienced the difference between Christ's peace and the world's peace?

ADD GOODNESS

Comfort each other and edify one another, just as you also are doing.

1 THESSALONIANS 5:11 NKJV

Instead of becoming dismayed by the chaos of world, we can remind one another of the better days which lie ahead. As Christians, we look forward to the day when Jesus returns and everything is made right. In the meantime, let us encourage one another and inspire each other to press on.

Marriage is filled with opportunities to encourage each other in your relationships with Jesus. You can embody the command to comfort and edify each other daily. You have unlimited access and influence with your spouse. Use your proximity to add goodness to their days.

How can you edify your spouse today?

FULFILLING THE LAW

Love does no wrong to a neighbor; therefore love is the fulfillment of the Law.

ROMANS 13:10 NASB

In the Old Testament, the law was emphasized in the lives of the Israelites. It was fulfilled by obedience, sacrifice, and adhering to God's standards. When Jesus died and rose again, he fulfilled the entirety of the law. His sacrifice became our eternal sacrifice. We no longer need to adhere to a specific set of rules in order to gain righteousness. Jesus is our righteous now and forever more.

In the same way, a good marriage is not about fulfilling burdensome requirements, intricate legalities, or endless rules. Marriage is about laying your lives down for each other. A successful marriage isn't built by both parties always doing the right thing. Instead, it is built by self-sacrifice and enduring love.

Is your marriage more focused on rules and keeping score than mutual self-sacrifice?

PRICE OF WISDOM

The beginning of wisdom is this: Get wisdom. Though it cost all you have, get understanding.

PROVERBS 4:7 NIV

This may seem like circular reasoning, but the insight included in these words are soul-saving. The first step to obtaining wisdom is to recognize the value in wisdom and our need for it. This understanding and eternal perspective requires a certain amount of wisdom initially. In other words, a wise person recognizes the value in wisdom and continues to search for it at any cost.

To be wise is far greater than to be rich, successful, well connected, or even happy. The good news is that there is no limit to how much wisdom you can have. God will give it to you eagerly every time you ask for it. He won't hold back, and he won't turn you away. He loves giving the gift of wisdom to his children!

What steps are you taking in your search for wisdom?

AUGUST

An enemy might defeat one person,
but two people together
can defend themselves;
a rope that is woven of three strings
is hard to break.

Ecclesiastes 4:12 NCV

EVER STRONGER

Be truly glad. There is wonderful joy ahead, even though you must endure many trials for a little while. These trials will show that your faith is genuine. It is being tested as fire tests and purifies gold—though your faith is far more precious than mere gold.

1 PETER 1:6-7 NLT

The paradox of our faith is that we can rejoice in our suffering and distress. The mystery of our call to glory is that we can celebrate our freedom in Christ while enduring trials and losses. The reason these impossibilities are real is because we have an unfailing hope in our eternal inheritance and the glorious redemption of our bodies through Jesus Christ our Lord.

Tough times are inevitable in any relationship. It takes perseverance and diligence to learn how to communicate well and navigate the trials of life as team. Hardships can rupture a relationship, or they can be used to initiate growth. Whatever you are facing, find God's peace and joy in the midst of it, and you will come through it stronger than ever.

What trials are you and your spouse facing right now? How can you endure together?

ENDURING LOVE

Give thanks to the God of heaven.
His faithful love endures forever.

PSALM 136:26 NLT

Who is in a better position to make an eternal promise than God? As the Creator of all, with a perfect record of upholding every promise he's ever made, the Lord is the most qualified entity to teach us what love and devotion mean.

As you lean into God's love and learn from his Scriptures, give thanks through prayer and praise. As you interact with him, let his love overflow to the people around you. This is what God desires most. His highest call is that you love him and love others. Your life will honor him when it is centered around those two things.

What are some practical ways to share God's unfailing love with your spouse?

TAKE NOTICE

He heals the brokenhearted and binds up their wounds.

PSALM 147:3 NIV

True love is compassionate and considerate. God expresses his love by binding up the wounds of the brokenhearted and healing their afflictions. He notices when people are hurting, and he actively does something about it. He is attentive, thoughtful, and capable of mending our brokenness.

When you think of love, this is what you should picture. Love is the decision to put someone else's needs ahead of your own. Noticing your spouse is one of the most basic ways to love them. Pay attention to them and offer your kindness, wisdom, or help when they need it. Thoughtfulness takes discipline and intentionality, but it reflects how God loves his people.

How can you show your spouse that you see them today?

FEAR GOD

Only fear the LORD and serve Him in truth with all your heart; for consider what great things He has done for you.

1 SAMUEL 12:24 NASB

God is so mighty. He spoke the very universe into existence. He created mankind, and he sustains us each day. He defeated massive armies with just a few faithful people. He sent his Son to earth and made a way for us to be redeemed. There is nothing he cannot do and no enemy he cannot defeat!

When you feel yourself forgetting God's faithfulness, read the Old Testament and be reminded. Look at Moses in Egypt, and the lengths God went to for his people to be freed. Consider Gideon, the shy man God used to defeat the Israelites' most powerful enemy of that time. Remember David, the shepherd that God used to take down a giant. He has faithfully intervened on behalf of his people for generations, and he won't stop now.

How have you seen God's faithfulness in your own life?

POSITIVE IMPACT

Just as each of us has one body with many members, and these members do not all have the same function, so in Christ we, though many, form one body, and each member belongs to all the others.

ROMANS 12:4-5 NIV

God made us to work together as a body not as separate entities. We each have an important part to play. When we combine our distinct roles, we have an opportunity to compensate for each other's weaknesses. We can use our strengths to life each other up. We honor the Lord when we work together as if we are one body.

You are part of something much bigger than yourself. You and your spouse are part of something much bigger than the two of you combined. Your actions, together and apart, have an impact beyond what you might see. Utilize your strengths for the good of those around you, and don't try to carry the burden of your weaknesses alone.

As a couple, how can you have a positive impact on your community?

ONE TEAM

No one is to seek his own advantage, but rather that of his neighbor.

1 Corinthians 10:24 NASB

Relationships do not thrive on keeping track or maintaining a fair score. Our interactions with God are not fair. Anyone who has children knows their relationship with them is not fair. Like any other relationship, marriage is not going to be fair one hundred percent of the time.

There is no room for self-centeredness in marriage. As a follower of Jesus, you are asked to lay your life down for your spouse. You are asked to love them even when you don't want to. Harboring offense, letting contempt grow in your heart, or allowing resentment to come between you won't create a flourishing marriage. Instead, embrace the truth that you will each give more than the other in various seasons and circumstances. Remember that you are a team, and you are not against each other.

How do you and your spouse approach the idea of fairness?

GOD'S PLANS

"I know the plans I have for you," declares the LORD, "plans to prosper you and not to harm you, plans to give you hope and a future."

JEREMIAH 29:11 NIV

Our perspective and expectations are typically flawed. We wish for things that will create happiness or satisfaction only to realize that the feeling is fleeting. We think we know what is best for us, and it's tempting to chase our flawed perception of goodness. Our ideas are not usually as incredible as we think they are.

In contrast, God's definition of goodness is perfect. He knows what's best for you, and he knows how to lead you down the right path. If you pursue his ways over your own, you will be satisfied. You won't be constantly searching for happiness because you'll carry contentment right in your heart. His plans are good, and they are filled with hope.

How have you seen God's plans play out in your life?

HE UNDERSTANDS

This High Priest of ours understands our weaknesses, for he faced all of the same testings we do, yet he did not sin. So let us come boldly to the throne of our gracious God. There we will receive his mercy, and we will find grace to help us when we need it most.

HEBREWS 4:15-16 NLT

Our confidence to approach God in prayer is not based on our own merit but on that of Jesus Christ. Nothing we have done allows us to boldly go before God. We can approach him because of what Jesus did for us on the cross. Because of him, we know we are washed clean, declared innocent, set free, and given access to Almighty God.

Isn't it a relief to know you can go to God any time you need his help and mercy? Jesus stood in the gap for you, and now there is nothing in the way of you experiencing God's perfect presence. Remember that you are never alone, and you are never expected to muster up enough strength for the day. God offers you everything you need through Jesus who understands your weaknesses.

Are there areas of your life where you've insisted on gritting your teeth and figuring it out alone?

GOOD REPUTATION

Encourage the young men to be self-controlled. In everything set them an example by doing what is good. In your teaching show integrity, seriousness and soundness of speech that cannot be condemned, so that those who oppose you may be ashamed because they have nothing bad to say about us.

TITUS 2:6-8 NIV

The way we live and the words we use should be an example to others of Biblical teachings and holy living. If our teaching is pure but our actions speak otherwise, we are hypocrites and untrustworthy. Our lifestyles should line up with our speech. What we say should be intentional and authentic.

Rather than being quick to offer your opinions and advice, it is important to exercise self-control and humility. In every area of life, Christians are called to demonstrate integrity and set an example for others. Regardless of whether other people praise your name or seek to shame you, your intention should be to live like Jesus did and point all honor back to him.

How can you and your spouse practice seriousness of speech?

NOT ALONE

These older women must train the younger women to love their husbands and their children, to live wisely and be pure, to work in their homes, to do good, and to be submissive to their husbands.

TITUS 2:4-5 NLT

There are multiple instances in the book of Titus where we see that the older generation is meant to teach the younger. Older women are encouraged to mentor new wives and mothers. Older men are told to share their wisdom with young men. This is a reminder that none of us are meant to navigate life alone. We need the help and encouragement of people who have gone before us.

You need the input of other people. It doesn't matter if you've been married for two years or twenty years. There will never be a point when you have learned it all. There will never be a time when you are released to depend upon your own understanding. There is maturity found in humility and the ability to learn from others. You were not designed to do it alone.

Do you and your spouse know an older couple you can trust and learn from?

TROUBLE AND HARDSHIP

Who shall separate us from the love of Christ? Shall trouble or hardship or persecution or famine or nakedness or danger or sword?

ROMANS 8:35 NIV

Some pain is the result of our own poor choices. Some hardships are a result of living in a broken world amongst sinful people. There will always be difficult situations that we don't understand yet long for an explanation. It's important to remember that answers might never come, but there is no trouble big enough to separate us from the love of God. He is dedicated be stay with us through every hardship.

As time goes by, it's easy to become more and more discouraged by the difficulties of life. Keep your heart turned toward the Lord so that bitterness and resentment won't build. Stay connected to him and remember that his love never fails. Ask him your questions without shame, and trust that he will faithfully lead you.

How can you encourage your spouse to remain in God's love even when life is disappointing?

CREATED WITH PURPOSE

Your eyes saw my unformed body;
all the days ordained for me were written in your book before one of them came to be.

PSALM 139:16 NIV

Each of us was created with a purpose. God displays himself through his handiwork, and he loves us like a perfect Father. Before we had even been formed, he already knew everything about us; he knew how we would look, who we would love, and what our struggles and strengths would be. He ordained every day of our lives, and he attentively watches over us.

Remember that your spouse was created with great care. They are precious in the eyes of God, and you are called to treat them as such. It's a gift to be given the opportunity to cherish someone who is so important to God. He has entrusted you with them, and he will equip you to love them just as he does. There are certain prayers that we can be assured God will answer. If you ask him to teach you how to love and cherish your spouse, he will do it.

What is one simple way you can treasure your spouse as much as God does?

GOD'S DIRECTIONS

I reach out for your commands, which I love,
that I may meditate on your decrees.

PSALM 119:48 NIV

The Lord has given us a set of laws to live by, and they offer guidance for every area of life. The world can be confusing, but we have the Holy Spirit to lead us and the Word of God to give us direction. We can confidently navigate our days because we know that God's commands are perfectly just and wise.

Many people hear of God's commandments and imagine a legalistic, perfectionistic dictator, but that is not who God is. His commandments are for your benefit, and they were created out of love. He loves you enough to hold you to a higher standard than the passing ways of this world. Reach out for God's commandments; fall in love with them. They are your lifeline and light in a dark world.

What does it look like to grow in affection for God's commands and decrees?

REFUSE TO ENGAGE

Accept the one whose faith is weak, without quarreling over disputable matters.

ROMANS 14:1 NIV

If our main takeaway from this verse is to consider ourselves strong and others weak, we miss the point. The point is acceptance, kindness, and the choice to not quarrel. Within our marriages, we often want to root out wrongness in our spouses at every opportunity. We see they hold a wrong opinion, and we confront them about it. We disagree with them on a minor point, and we push to make our own voice heard. This verse from Paul is for times like these.

You get to choose if you will communicate with grace or pride. If being right is your highest value, it might be time to evaluate your heart. Winning an argument is a fleeting prize. You'll find temporary gain at a larger cost than you might realize. Instead, refuse to engage in meaningless debates and use your words to lift others up.

How can you combat the desire to be right?

WORTHY LIVING

I, the prisoner of the Lord, urge you to walk in a manner worthy of the calling with which you have been called.

EPHESIANS 4:1 NASB

Our marriages are included in the call us to live in a way that reflects the character and purpose of Christ. How we treat each other as married people must reflect the faith we profess. Marriage is part of the ministry that is our lives, and it impacts the world around us. This is especially true in a time when marriage has become more of an afterthought than a lifelong commitment.

Your marriage is more important than you might think. It's about more than just you and your partner. Your love for each other is meant to teach the world around you about Christ's love for the church. Your failures and successes reflect on the entire body of Christ. This is a high calling which should be treated with respect.

What impact does your particular marriage have on the body of Christ?

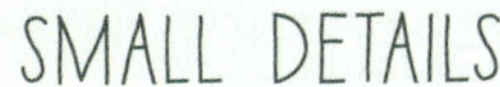

SMALL DETAILS

"Do not worry about your life, what you will eat or drink; or about your body, what you will wear. Is not life more than food, and the body more than clothes? Look at the birds of the air; they do not sow or reap or store away in barns, and yet your heavenly Father feeds them. Are you not much more valuable than they?"

MATTHEW 6:25-26 NIV

As is always the case with the Jesus, he cautioned his listeners to stop worrying and keep trusting that God is good, faithful, and generous. Even the birds are fed and provided for. Christ is not advocating for carelessness or irresponsibility, but he is warning us not to obsess over money or material possessions.

Let your work be an act of worship toward the Lord rather than a frantic pursuit for more. Remember that he is the one who sustains you. He has given you skills, talents, and opportunities. Your life is securely in his hands, and he doesn't want you to fret over the details. Put your worries in his hands and let him order your steps.

Are you or your spouse working in a way that is detrimental to your relationships and health?

GRATITUDE

The generous soul will be made rich,
And he who waters will also be watered himself.

PROVERBS 11:25 NKJV

All generosity is born out of gratitude, for no one can give without acknowledging they have enough. The most generous are the most grateful; they understand how much they've been blessed and want to bless others in turn.

Generosity is a skill that must be cultivated. You and your spouse get to decide if you will be cheerful givers or not. You get to choose how you live and how much you will offer to those around you. Don't give because you feel obligated but do it because you are thankful for all the Lord has done for you. Open your hands and experience the joy of lifting others up.

What are some habits you can change in order to be more generous?

PEACE IN HUMILITY

Humble yourselves under the mighty power of God, and at the right time he will lift you up in honor. Give all your worries and cares to God, for he cares about you.

1 PETER 5:6-7 NLT

We all crave significance and recognition. This desire isn't wrong, but it becomes a problem when we misplace the source. God promises to lift us up as we follow him. He honors those who humble themselves. Seeking to honor ourselves is the opposite of humility. Searching for recognition on our own only deprives us of the real deal.

The praises of others will never satisfy your desire for approval. Earthly praise brings momentary satisfaction, but it won't do anything for your soul. Don't look for approval from the people around you when they don't have the authority to give it to you. Trust the Lord, follow his ways, and he will lift you up at the right time. His honor is far better than any accolades you could find on your own.

Do you trust that God is more than enough to fill your heart and satisfy your soul?

MOTIVATION

Let us think of ways to motivate one another to acts of love and good works.

HEBREWS 10:24 NLT

As citizens of the kingdom of God, we have a bigger role to play than simply being concerned with our own well-being. We are instructed to help our brothers and sisters in Christ and look for ways to motivate them toward love and good works. We are to care for each other because God cares for us.

Marriage is a fantastic way to live out this calling. Each day is filled with chances to love, encourage, motivate, bless, and care for your spouse. You can motivate your spouse effectively because you know them better than anyone else. When your marriage is strong, even more opportunities open up for to influence the world around you together.

How can you encourage your spouse toward acts of love and good works?

BY GOD'S GRACE

By the grace of God I am what I am, and his grace toward me was not in vain. On the contrary, I worked harder than any of them, though it was not I, but the grace of God that is with me.

1 CORINTHIANS 15:10 ESV

Paul had an impressive resume. He had many reasons to boast, and the people around him knew of his long list of accomplishments. He knew that he could have easily convinced people that he did everything by his own merit. It wouldn't have been a difficult debate. This is why it was so meaningful when Paul declared that God's grace was the reason for his transformation.

When pride wells up within you, that is the most important time to give God the credit. When you are tempted to stand upon your own success, remember Paul's example. Deliberately lift up the name of the Lord and humbly remember the grace he has given you. You are where you are because of him.

In what area of your life can you practice giving God the credit rather than taking it yourself?

STAND FIRM

Be alert and of sober mind. Your enemy the devil prowls around like a roaring lion looking for someone to devour. Resist him, standing firm in the faith, because you know that the family of believers throughout the world is undergoing the same kind of suffering.

1 Peter 5:8-9 NIV

We cannot give our lives to Jesus and then coast through life. We are not meant to be idle as we follow him along the narrow road to eternal life. Peter warns us of the trials we will have, and if we heed his words, we will have no reason to be surprised by the presence of the trials. Life will be hard at times, but we are not alone in our suffering.

Your faith requires action. Scripture is clear that you must resist temptation, stand firm, and stay alert. Thankfully, God does not call you to these things then leave you stranded. The Holy Spirit is your source of strength and power. He is the reason you can have the mind of Christ and follow in his footsteps with confident assurance.

How have you and your spouse experienced the leadership of the Holy Spirit?

OUR BEST LIFE

"What does the Lord your God ask of you but to fear the Lord your God, to walk in obedience to him, to love him, to serve the Lord your God with all your heart and with all your soul?"

Deuteronomy 10:12 NIV

We often overcomplicate the idea of following God's will. We fret about the path we are on, and we worry that we've missed God's plan for our lives. We mull over every possibility as if we are in control, and we try to muster up the right circumstances as if we can manipulate God's hand. The truth is that he has clearly communicated his will.

God asks you to love him and serve him. It's true that everyone will interpret that in different ways, but your heart is what matters most. If your desire is to honor him, and you humbly offer him your life, you will not go astray. Stay connected to him through the Spirit, and he will not let you down.

What does it look like for you to serve God with all your heart in this season of life?

SLEEP IN PEACE

I go to bed and sleep in peace,
because, Lord, only you keep me safe.

Psalm 4:8 NCV

There was always uncertainty and danger in David's life, yet the one thing he was certain about was that his God loved him and would always be watching out for him. In his heart he had the peace of God, so he was able to unplug from the day's drama and sleep soundly.

Nighttime is the perfect time for your mind to race and your thoughts to get jumbled. There are probably particular worries that keep you awake from time to time. Maybe you have financial stress, or maybe there's a relationship in your life that is strained. Whatever your worries are, remember that God will sustain you. He sees what plagues you, and he longs to give you rest.

How can you and your spouse combat nighttime worries?

GUARD YOUR MOUTH

One who guards his mouth and his tongue,
Guards his soul from troubles.

PROVERBS 21:23 NASB

Guarding our tongues requires humility, self-control, awareness, and a whole lot of prayer. As messengers and ambassadors of God, we need to train our tongues and guard our mouths. What we say may have a greater impact for either good or evil than we realize.

How often have your words gotten you into trouble? Perhaps you recently insulted your partner on purpose or accidentally. Maybe you love to win arguments, or you need to have the last word. Whatever your habits are, remember that your words are like fire. They can provide warmth and comfort, or they can cause destruction and pain. Choose caution over carelessness.

Is there a habit of speech God might be asking you to change?

HUMBLE LOVE

Always be humble and gentle. Be patient with each other, making allowance for each other's faults because of your love.

EPHESIANS 4:2 NLT

Failure to show humility and gentleness to each other in our weaknesses can lead to strife. This strife can make marriages fail, churches split, and friends begrudgingly part ways. Making allowances for people does not mean excusing sin, but it does mean we should show grace because God showed us grace.

If you have been married for any amount of time, you know your spouse has faults, and they know you have them too. Being married as imperfect partners can easily result in grudges, or resentment, but that is not what God wants for your marriage. He wants you to experience the joy of a partnership that is defined by kindness and encouragement.

When your spouse falls short of your expectations, how can you remain humble and loving while showing them grace and patience?

GRATEFUL TOGETHER

In everything give thanks; for this is the will of God in Christ Jesus for you.

1 THESSALONIANS 5:18 NKJV

Although we may not feel grateful during difficult seasons, our lives are still filled with reasons to give thanks to God. He is still on the throne, redeeming the lost, blessing the faithful, and loving us unconditionally. He remains the same despite our circumstances. Finding reasons to praise him in every season will help us develop endurance, strength of character, and unshakeable faith.

Whether you have a good or bad week, you have the same God who uses all circumstances for your growth and his glory. Begin practicing gratitude with your husband or wife. Learn how to remind each other of the good things in your life. It might feel silly or trite at first, but this habit will grow, and your heart will soften. Noticing God's goodness is always worth it.

How can you gently remind each other of God's goodness when life is hard?

FRUITFUL

"I am the vine, you are the branches. He who abides in Me, and I in him, bears much fruit; for without Me you can do nothing."

JOHN 15:5 NKJV

A fruitful life and marriage are desirable, but the only way they happen is if we're plugged in to the source of growth. A branch can't produce fruit by lying on the ground by itself. If we want a healthy, thriving marriage, it's going to require a healthy connection to Jesus.

Stay connected to the vine. Be nourished by the presence of Jesus and let his guiding hand shape your life, heart, and home. Good things come from abiding in him. Scripture says that as you remain in him, he will fill your life with love, joy, peace, patience, kindness, goodness, faithfulness, gentleness, and self-control. Imagine having a life and marriage that are fully defined by those characteristics!

Are you connected to the vine, or are you trying to navigate your life and marriage apart from him?

DISTINCTLY UNIQUE

"I will make him a helper fit for him."

GENESIS 2:18 ESV

From the very beginning God declared that women were meant to be helpers. If we look at the translation of the word helper, we can see that it's the same word used to describe God's help toward mankind. This tells us that being a helper is not subservient or less important. A wife's role is not diminutive. She is man's helper because she brings strength to the table.

How do you define the roles in your marriage? God does not condone anyone being treated as lesser than. He did not create women to be overlooked and undervalued. A godly husband highly esteems his wife. A godly wife is in a powerful position to lift up her husband. When the two work together and love each other selflessly, God is glorified.

How can you use your strength to be a blessing to your spouse?

BIGGER PICTURE

We know that in all things God works for the good of those who love him, who have been called according to his purpose.

ROMANS 8:28 NIV

Following God does not mean things will go smoothly all the time. It does mean that he will work for our good. We can trust him even when our circumstances seem impossible. He sees what we don't, and he knows how to intertwine all the details of our lives. His perception is goodness is so much better than our own.

If your path today is grim, trust in the one who has a perfect bird's-eye view. He can see the bigger picture, and he knows exactly what each of your days will look like. You can put your life in his hands and trust that he won't lead you astray. He is capable of taking your darkest moments and using them for his glory and your good.

How can you and your spouse trust that God is working in your current circumstances?

AUGUST 30

ENDURING HOPE

Hope does not disappoint, because the love of God has been poured out in our hearts by the Holy Spirit who was given to us.

ROMANS 5:5 NKJV

Hope is the driving force behind our life choices and commitments. We hope for better days, for good to reign, and for eternal life with no stain of sin. A marriage between believers is based on this sort of hope, and a union centered on God will grow stronger each day. The Lord instills hope in our hearts and fills us with love and faith. When we encounter despair, the Holy Spirit reminds us hope which will last longer than pain.

Your hope is not strong because of your own abilities or steadfastness. Your hope is strong because God is trustworthy. He always keeps his promises, and he has promised to never leave you. He has promised to love you through life's trials, and he has promised to come back and make everything right.

How can you hold onto hope today?

DIVINELY SANCTIONED

"What therefore God has joined together, let not man separate."

MARK 10:9 ESV

Marriage is not a human concept. It's God's idea, and God's plan for marriage is both a blessing and a challenge. The world might be casual toward marriage, but God takes it seriously. He is clear that our vows should be honored, and he promises to equip us to do it.

It's common for spouses to take each other for granted. As your marriage grows in longevity, don't let it fade in commitment. Be somber toward your vows and take them seriously. Remember that you made a covenant before God, and honoring your spouse honors him. Repeat your promises to your spouse and hold yourself to a high standard. Protect your marriage and treat it as the precious gift it is.

How can you more fully honor the covenant you made to your spouse before God?

SEPTEMBER

Do not owe anyone anything, except to love one another, for the one who loves another has fulfilled the law.

Romans 13:8 CSB

TEMPTATION

Let no one say when he is tempted, "I am tempted by God"; for God cannot be tempted by evil, nor does He Himself tempt anyone.

JAMES 1:13 NKJV

God does not tempt his children. He does not dangle sin in front of us while waiting for us to fail. He does not exploit our weaknesses or take advantage of our failures. He is a good Father who longs to equip, comfort, and teach us. If we attribute the temptation in our lives to God, we are missing major aspects of his character.

God does not ask you to grit your teeth and see how long you can withstand evil. He gives you the tools you need to resist and flee. He offers you opportunities to say no to temptation, and he gives you grace to make wise choices. Stay connected to your good Father, and he will guide you.

What are practical ways you resist temptation in your own life?

RESPONDING TO MERCY

I urge you, brothers and sisters, in view of God's mercy, to offer your bodies as a living sacrifice, holy and pleasing to God—this is your true and proper worship.

ROMANS 12:1 NIV

Paul explained that true worship is offering ourselves in service to God as if we were living sacrifices for him. Praise and worship are our purpose. What better purpose could there be? We get the honor of living for something beyond this temporary existence. God granted us mercy so we could be part of his great work on the earth. What a generous gift and calling!

How has God asked you to live? Everyone's answer might vary slightly, and it's important to acknowledge your own obedience to his call. It doesn't matter what the person or couple next to you is doing. What matters most is your own sacrifice toward the Lord.

How have you offered your own life and marriage to the one who created you?

ALWAYS HEARD

I love the LORD, because he has heard my voice
and my pleas for mercy.
Because he inclined his ear to me,
therefore I will call on him as long as I live.

PSALM 116:1-2 ESV

We serve a God who hears us. We have his attention, and he longs for us to know that he sees us. After all, his attentiveness and mercy are what set him apart. He is kind, compassionate, and he loves his children well. He does not withhold his voice in anger, and he does not ignore us when we are hurting. His ear is inclined toward us, and we can trust that he will answer when we call upon him.

God speaks to you. He might not say what you want, and he might communicate differently than you expect, but he is speaking. His Word is living and active, his Spirit faithfully testifies of his character, and creation declares his majesty. You do not serve a silent God. He is not ignoring you, and he is not unmoved by your plights. He sees you, and you can rely on him.

Do you genuinely believe that God hears you? How does this impact your prayers?

A GOD DECISION

I will instruct you and teach you
in the way you should go;
I will counsel you with my loving eye on you.

PSALM 32:8 NIV

God's love for us is great. He is a kind Father who loves to teach his children. He is happy to show us which way to go, and he enjoys being involved in our lives. If we take the time to listen, we will find that he is always speaking.

Open your heart to receive the Lord's lessons, and he will faithfully instruct you. He will increase your understanding when you humbly seek his ways. He does not hide his face from you but keeps his gaze upon you because you are his beloved child. He is a good teacher and the best mentor.

What has the Lord been teaching you recently?

INFLUENCE

Blessed is the one who does not
walk in step with the wicked
or stand in the way that sinners take
or sit in the company of mockers,
but whose delight is in the law of the LORD,
and who meditates on his law day and night.

PSALM 1:1-2 NIV

The people we surround ourselves with have a great influence on our lives whether we notice it or not. The words we hear regularly and the attitudes demonstrated by those we spend time with have a significant impact on us. This is why the author of this passage emphasized choosing friends wisely. If we choose friends who reject truth and righteousness, we will have a near-impossible time remaining on solid ground.

What are the strongest influences in your marriage? Where do you and your spouse seek wisdom, comfort, and companionship? It's important to recognize that you will become like the people or content you surround yourself with. Find friendships, mentors, and habits that reflect the law of the Lord.

Are the influences you and your spouse allow into your lives drawing you closer to Christ?

IN THE MORNING

LORD, every morning you hear my voice.
Every morning, I tell you what I need,
and I wait for your answer.

PSALM 5:3 NCV

When David went before God in prayer every morning, he did so with confidence that God heard him and would answer. Our prayers are not empty, one-way conversations. They are not simply symbolic gestures of spiritualism. When we pray, we are talking directly to the almighty maker of heaven and earth, and he hears us.

Your Father listens to our prayers, knows your needs, and answers you. His answers are not always what you would like or were expecting, but they are always based out of love and wisdom. His vantagepoint is higher than yours, and he understands the bigger picture of your life. You can approach him boldly and with confidence because he knows what is best.

Do you take time every morning to pray to God? Do you leave time to pause and listen for a response?

GAZING HEAVENWARD

If then you have been raised with Christ, seek the things that are above, where Christ is, seated at the right hand of God.

COLOSSIANS 3:1 ESV

When Christ died, we were buried with him and permanently severed from sin. When Christ rose from the dead, we were also raised out of darkness and into newness of life. Because we trust in the Lord as our Savior and accept his gift of salvation, we are forever united with him, and a seat is reserved for us in his kingdom.

Your choices make a difference, and today's verse is a reminder that you get to choose what you seek. It's an exhortation to seek the things above, where Christ is, rather than the temporary things on earth. Keep your eyes on Jesus, and you won't go astray.

What are you actively seeking today?

HAPPY DAYS

There is a time to cry and a time to laugh.
There is a time to be sad and a time to dance.

ECCLESIASTES 3:4 NCV

God does not expect us to remain positive all the time. He does not ask us to put on a happy face and pretend like everything is easy. He knows full well that life is filled with many seasons. His promise is that he will remain with us through all of it. He is with us when we cry, and he is with us when we dance.

If Scripture acknowledges the full spectrum of human emotions, so can you. There is freedom in recognizing that there is a season for everything. Sometimes life deals you heartache, and it's not fruitful to deny it. Sometimes life feels incredibly beautiful, and it's okay to embrace it. God is with you at all times and in the midst of every emotion.

Are you in a season of laughing or crying? Are you comfortable being where God has you?

EYES ON HIM

I keep my eyes always on the LORD.
With him at my right hand, I will not be shaken.

PSALM 16:8 NIV

When we keep our eyes on the Lord, the worries of this life seem less catastrophic. Focusing on him doesn't mean we are unaware of what's going on around us, but it means that we are giving our attention to the right thing. If we spend all our time dwelling on our problems, they will surely become more and more impactful. If we turn our gaze toward our Maker, our steps will be steady.

Looking to the Lord is like a reflex. It's a muscle you can train and a habit you can develop. Remind yourself over and over to look his way. Give him your attention. Call upon his name. Thank him for his many blessings. The more you look to him, the more you will see that he has always been faithful, and he won't stop now.

What helps you remember to look to the Lord?

TRAINED FOR BATTLE

God arms me with strength,
and he makes my way perfect.
He makes me as surefooted as a deer,
enabling me to stand on mountain heights.
He trains my hands for battle;
he strengthens my arm to draw a bronze bow.

PSALM 18:32-34 NLT

David was a well-known war hero who overthrew his enemy countless times. Without fail, he always attributed his victories to God. He knew that it was God who had equipped him for battle. God gave him the strength and courage he needed, and it was for God's glory that he fought.

God is with you through every battle you face. He equips you, and he offers you his strength. He makes you surefooted even in environments where you would expect to falter. He knows exactly what you need, and he is fully capable of giving it to you. He invites you to step forward in confidence, knowing that he has gone before you and will remain by your side.

What battles are you and your spouse facing? How has he trained you to fight them?

FULLY EQUIPPED

He has told you, O man, what is good;
and what does the LORD require of you
but to do justice, and to love kindness,
and to walk humbly with your God?

MICAH 6:8 ESV

We complicate our theology all too often. We debate little details with little eternal significance. We try so hard to fit God into our own ideas, perceptions, and preferences. God, however, has made his will clear. He asks us to do justice, love kindness, and walk humbly. These standards matter far more than our debates.

The difficulty is not in understanding God's commandments but in following them. The good news of the gospel is that through Christ's death and resurrection, you have everything you need to please God. He has equipped you to live exactly as he's called you to. Christ's love is the reason you can love justice, choose kindness, and walk humbly with God.

How are you applying God's commands to your marriage?

FLOURISHING

I am like an olive tree flourishing in the house of God; I trust in God's unfailing love for ever and ever.

PSALM 52:8 NIV

Something that flourishes is not just doing well; it's doing extremely well. It's wonderful to have a flourishing marriage. There isn't an exact formula to having a flourishing marriage, but one of the best paths to ensure it is to put God at the center. God's unfailing love will forever be the answer to a successful marriage.

A healthy tree has deep roots that can absorb nutrients and keep the plant steady when storms come. Your marriage is similar. If you want it to be healthy, it must be rooted in the love of God. His love is the sustenance your marriage needs, and his love will keep you firmly in place when trials threaten to overwhelm you.

In what ways are you intentionally nurturing your marriage with God's love?

GOD'S COMMANDMENTS

This is the love of God, that we keep his commandments. And his commandments are not burdensome.

1 John 5:3 ESV

God's love and his commandments are intricately intertwined. To show the love of God, we must keep his commandments. God's commandments are more than a set of dos and don'ts, and their purpose is not simply to lead us to repentance; they teach us how to love. His commandments mold us into people who love like Jesus loves.

Following God's commandments is how we love him, and following his commandments is not burdensome. Living a life that honors the Lord is not meant to be complicated, impossible, or out of reach. He is not a tyrant who expects us to strictly adhere or else; he is a Father who is faithful to comfort and guide his children.

How might your perspective change if you saw God's commands as life giving rather than burdensome commands?

TRUE VALUABLES

"Sell your possessions and give to the poor. Provide purses for yourselves that will not wear out, a treasure in heaven that will never fail, where no thief comes near and no moth destroys. For where your treasure is, there your heart will be also."

LUKE 12:33-34 NIV

God wants us to be good stewards of the resources he puts in our hands. The land around us, the wealth we accumulate, and the possessions we have all belong to him. He wants us to know that no matter the amount of money in our retirement account, it is ultimately fleeting and worthless.

Generosity, compassion, love, and commitment are investments that will last into eternity. When you and your spouse value the things of God, you will find that your hearts belong to God. As you devote yourselves to collecting eternal treasures, you will find satisfaction and joy that goes beyond momentary earthly pleasures.

In what ways can you value eternal treasures over earthly ones?

GODLY CONTENTMENT

There is great gain in godliness with contentment, for we brought nothing into the world, and we cannot take anything out of the world. But if we have food and clothing, with these we will be content.

1 TIMOTHY 6:6-8 ESV

Contentment is paramount for a person who is living for God and not themselves. We came into this world with nothing, and we will leave it with nothing as well. Spending our days chasing wealth is a waste of life that could be devoted to something meaningful and eternal. The Bible does not speak against having wealth, but it warns against allowing it to become your master and primary pursuit.

The world will tell you that you deserve to fill your life with a collection of things that make you happy. You are promised that rewarding yourself for your hard work is the best way to reduce stress. The truth is that joy and satisfaction come primarily from God's presence. Seek him, and you will find what you are looking for.

What has God given to you and your spouse that you are thankful for today?

POWER OF UNITY

Two people are better off than one,
for they can help each other succeed.

ECCLESIASTES 4:9 NLT

Two are better than one. When a problem arises and you're working alone, it can quickly become overwhelming and discouraging. Burdens lighten when someone else helps you carry them. We are stronger together than we are apart.

God knew this when he designed marriage. What an incredible gift to have someone by your side through life's highs and lows! Unity within marriage makes life richer and more fulfilling than a marriage simply comprised of two individuals living their own lives. Learn to walk together, leaning on each other, and embracing life's many seasons as one.

How can you help your spouse succeed today?

GENTLE ANSWER

A gentle answer will calm a person's anger,
but an unkind answer will cause more anger.

PROVERBS 15:1 NCV

It is one thing to be right, and another thing to create change. By insensitively asserting ourselves, even if we are justified in what we are saying, we may lose more than we gain. Angry debates and pride don't lead to change. In contrast, kindness and patience create peace.

Patience and kindness within marriage must be cultivated. These are habits that take practice and humility. They are fruit of the Spirit that come from abiding in Christ. As you grow in love, you will inevitably grow in other areas. Submit yourself to the Lord and allow him to help you develop character that honors him.

When you and your spouse disagree, how can you talk it through without anger taking over?

EVERLASTING IMPACT

We fix our eyes not on what is seen, but on what is unseen, since what is seen is temporary, but what is unseen is eternal.

2 Corinthians 4:18 NIV

It's easy to become overwhelmed by the trials of life. Seemingly urgent matters hang over our heads like tyrants. We worry about bills, schedules, jobs, and projects. We are constantly accomplishing more but rarely feel successful. This is because we were not designed to focus on what is easily seen. God created us to fix our eyes on what is unseen.

Your life is about so much more than the physical, tangible things you can see. Your primary goal is to love God and love his people. If you spend all of your time, energy, and money doing that, you will not be disappointed. Though you can't see them now, the eternal treasures found in his kingdom are well worth everything you have.

How can you shift your focus from what is seen to the unseen?

REWARDS

"I the Lord search the heart and examine the mind, to reward each person according to their conduct, according to what their deeds deserve."

Jeremiah 17:10 NIV

God is omniscient. This means that he knows everything. He sees the deepest corners of our hearts and the most fleeting thoughts that cross our minds. He knows our strongest desires, greatest weaknesses, and biggest secrets. He understands our intentions, knows our motivations, and isn't surprised by our thought processes.

God knows everything about you. This is not meant to cause shame or embarrassment. Instead, it can give you confidence. He loves you with full knowledge of your weakness and sin. You don't need to hide from him or offer him a curated version of yourself. Offer him your authentic heart and allow him to transform it.

How does God's omniscience impact the way you approach him?

LOVING THE VISIBLE

If someone says, "I love God," and yet he hates his brother or sister, he is a liar; for the one who does not love his brother and sister whom he has seen, cannot love God, whom he has not seen.

1 John 4:20 NASB

It's important for our words to line up with our actions. Once we say our marriage vows, we are committed to upholding them. We must love our spouse in word and deed. Our love should go beyond liking the idea of them or wanting to enjoy the benefits of marriage. We are called to lay our lives down each day. Our love for each other shows that we love God.

If we hate the visible people around us, then we cannot love the invisible God. We put his love into practice through our love of the people around us. Devotion to a real, regular person is what genuine, heartfelt commitment looks like. Loving each other despite weakness isn't easy, but it is worth it.

How can you make amends for areas of life where your actions haven't lined up with your words?

WEIGHTY MATTERS

A man who makes a vow to the Lord or makes a pledge under oath must never break it. He must do exactly what he said he would do.

Numbers 30:2 NLT

Marriage has been trivialized in modern society, and even believers can lose sight of the value God has placed on it. Covenants are important and are meant to be taken seriously. Marriage needs to be respected by all parties, and we should always have the intention of honoring the vows we spoke to each other before God and witnesses.

Your vows are not meant to be diminished by time or trials. Covenants are made to withstand the highs and lows of life. If you expect your commitment to remain unchallenged, you'll set yourself up for disappointment. Remind yourself that conflict, trials, and hardships don't get to decide the strength of your marriage. Your response matters more than your circumstances.

How might you honor your marriage vows in the face of unmet expectations?

EACH HAS A GIFT

If your gift is to encourage others, be encouraging. If it is giving, give generously. If God has given you leadership ability, take the responsibility seriously. And if you have a gift for showing kindness to others, do it gladly.

Romans 12:8 NLT

Our Father is wonderfully creative, and he loves displaying it. Each of us have been given different gifts to use in service to one another. Any time a believer has a God-given talent or skill, the Bible makes it clear that the purpose of it is not for the elevation of the individual but the betterment of the church body.

Using your gifts takes practice and faith. It is God alone who can cause new life and growth, but you must be faithful to step out and use what he has trusted you with. Take time to nurture your gifts and encourage your spouse's gifts. You know each other better than anyone else, and you can help each other identify and then embrace your God given gifts.

What gifts have you been given? What gifts does your spouse have?

BE KIND

Be kind to one another, compassionate, forgiving each other, just as God in Christ also has forgiven you.

EPHESIANS 4:32 NASB

Christians are part of a single, unified family. We each operate differently within the body of Christ. We all have different roles and varying gifts. For the body of believers to work well together, we need to be kind and compassionate despite our differences. We need to be forgiving. When that's difficult, we can remember we have been forgiven by Christ first.

A lot of conflict begins with unmet expectations. We have an idea of how people should behave, and we are let down when they don't measure up. What might happen if we gave each other the freedom to operate according to God's will and not our personal expectations? We honor the Lord when we embrace compassion and forgiveness rather than insisting on our own preferences or ideas.

Do you have any unspoken expectations of your spouse?

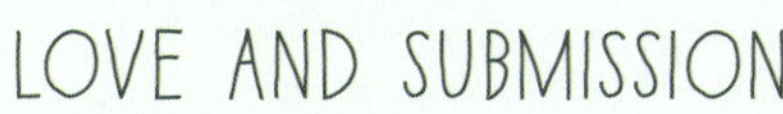

LOVE AND SUBMISSION

Wives, be subject to your husbands, as is fitting in the Lord. Husbands, love your wives and do not become bitter against them.

COLOSSIANS 3:18-19 NASB

God is always calling us to higher maturity. Marriage is designed to bless us and also push us to a spiritually deeper way of living. The Bible instructs wives to cooperate in helping their husbands, and for husbands to sacrificially love their wives. This is a relationship defined by mutual submission and selfless love. Both parties are expected to lay down their lives.

It's been said that a healthy marriage is a race to the bottom. When you and your wife are both seeking to serve each other, the idea of submission or authority isn't controversial or messy. Your marriage isn't meant to be a one-sided exchange where one person constantly benefits over the other. You are each called to lift up the other in loving kindness.

In what ways are you actively laying down your life for your spouse?

AUTHORITY

Remind the people to be subject to rulers and authorities, to be obedient, to be ready to do whatever is good, to slander no one, to be peaceable and considerate, and always to be gentle toward everyone.

Titus 3:1-2 NIV

We may disagree with things our leaders say or do, but there is a way to discuss them without slander. They are under God too, and they will answer to him in the end. We are called to guard our words and trust God's judgment rather than letting evil speech seep out of our mouths.

It's not difficult to rant and rave about your opinion. It's easy to become angry or frustrated when you look at the state of the world. God calls you to be peaceful despite the chaos that surrounds you. He calls you to be considerate and gentle toward everyone despite how they behave toward you. What you say matters because it reveals the condition of your heart.

How can your household embrace the challenge found in today's Scripture?

FACING TROUBLE

The righteous person faces many troubles,
but the LORD comes to the rescue each time.

PSALM 34:19 NLT

Sometimes things go wrong, and we are left wondering why. Despite our prayers and fasting, despite our service to the Lord, we still endure troubles and are faced with disappointments like everyone else. It has often been asked why bad things happen to good people. Why does God allow it to rain on the just and the unjust alike?

King David's psalm offers encouragement for these times. Even though you face difficulties and afflictions, you can trust Yahweh to deliver you no matter the depth of the issue. You are God's child, and he will always come through for you. He is faithful to intervene on your behalf even when you don't see it. Your circumstances might seem desperate, but you are not alone.

What difficulty are you and your spouse facing right now that you would like to pray for God's deliverance from?

WATCH YOUR WORDS

If anyone thinks he is religious and does not bridle his tongue but deceives his heart, this person's religion is worthless.

JAMES 1:26 ESV

Words can build, and words can destroy. We need to be extremely careful about what words we put in the air. This is especially true within marriage. What we say and how we say it reflects what is inside our hearts. Our speech betrays our spiritual condition. Our words are a good gauge for where our hearts truly lie.

Perhaps you think you're doing well because you're adhering to religious niceties, but have you been getting angry easily? Are you complaining a lot? Do you gossip about other people or slander them? Are you always pointing out the negative first? Pay close attention to the fruit of your words. Use them to life up, encourage, and create.

What do your recent words to your spouse reveal about your heart?

UNAFRAID

I will not be afraid, because the Lord is with me. People can't do anything to me

Psalm 118:6 NCV

From time-to-time fear gets the best of us. Fear can hijack our minds and drive us away from trusting God. It prompts us to rely on our own strength, forsaking the wisdom and power of the Almighty. When tragedy overtakes us or imposing threats wreak havoc on our hearts, it is easy to take our gaze off God and replace our faith with fear.

God's Word assures you that he is always with you, and you need not be fearful. He has given you the Holy Spirit who offers you peace instead of fear. When fear arises, you can submit your heart to your Maker and trust that he sees beyond your current circumstances. He holds each of your days in his loving hands.

Do you have any fears you need to lay before the Lord?

LOYAL FRIENDS

A friend loves at all times,
and a brother is born for a time of adversity.

PROVERBS 17:17 NIV

Friendship within marriage can be a great blessing. Not every couple describes themselves as best friends, and that's okay. It's okay if you and your spouse don't have the same hobbies or interests. The call to friendship goes far beyond how you spend your time. A good friend is kind, patient, and understanding. A good friend is thoughtful, available, and helpful.

Have you been a good friend to your spouse? Are you reliable in times of need? Are you mindful of their emotions and opinions? Take time to nurture your friendship. Spend quality time together and remember the things you love most about your partner. When you choose to loyally stick together and serve God side by side through good and hard times, a deep friendship is bound to bloom.

How can you cultivate your friendship with your spouse today?

IMITATE GOD

Imitate God, therefore, in everything you do, because you are his dear children.

EPHESIANS 5:1 NLT

Children begin imitating their parents as soon as they learn to talk, and they keep imitating them, either consciously or subconsciously, for the rest of their lives. If we are God's children, we will follow God's example. That means not taking part in actions, attitudes, and motives that are unacceptable to God. It means embracing his perspective and opinions in all we do.

You are dear to God, and he cares about your growth. He wants to see you live abundantly, and he knows that is accomplished by following the path he has for you. He doesn't ask you to imitate him out of pride or vanity. He knows that you will find the most satisfaction, joy, and sense of belonging by embracing the way of your Maker.

In what ways do you feel called to imitate God in this season?

OCTOBER

Love is patient, love is kind. It does not envy, it does not boast, it is not proud.

1 Corinthians 13:4 NIV

REPLACING ASHES

"I will give them a crown to replace their ashes,
and the oil of gladness to replace their sorrow,
and clothes of praise to replace their spirit of sadness."

ISAIAH 61:3 NCV

Although we live in a broken world, God promises that we will still experience goodness. He fills us with hope as we cling to his promises. He assures us that he will turn our tears into dancing, and our morning into shouts of joy! We can rest in the fact that whatever happens, no matter how dark our surroundings become, we have a future of goodness and light waiting for us.

Do not despair if you are experiencing hardships, it does not mean God has forsaken you. Hold onto the truth that he will give you a new life and that the evil of this world will pass away. He does not intend for his children to suffer forever. He will put an end to your grief, and a new season will come.

Can you imagine a love so strong that it can replace all your sorrow with joy in a single moment?

GOD'S FAITHFULNESS

"Know therefore that the LORD your God is God; he is the faithful God, keeping his covenant of love to a thousand generations of those who love him and keep his commandments."

DEUTERONOMY 7:9 NIV

Many of us have insurance for our houses, cars, or health. The main purpose of insurance is to confirm that help will be there when we need it most. God also works to hedge against unforeseen difficulties, but his insurance is so much better than anything we can produce on our own. His promises never fail, and we cannot do anything to earn them.

God's promises are your best insurance. He is faithful, good, and kind. It is better to depend on his promises than your own perception. Learn to lean on him and you will be less likely to waver in times of trouble.

Where do you and your spouse find your greatest sense of security?

OUR STRUGGLE

Our struggle is not against flesh and blood, but against the rulers, against the powers, against the world forces of this darkness, against the spiritual forces of wickedness in the heavenly places.

EPHESIANS 6:12 NASB

As we consider the condition of the world, it is easy to become fixated on the enemies we can see. Those who prey on the vulnerable, who exploit others for gain, who take pleasure in the suffering of others can seem like our most impending adversaries. Our actual enemy, the ruler of darkness, is the one who influences people to sin and who works them into his own evil ploys.

Consider the bigger picture before becoming too focused on the physical enemies you can see. Remember that you and your spouse are not enemies. You are on the same team, and you have a mutual adversary who would love to see your marriage fail. It's easy to think that your battles are with each other, but unity is found when you face problems hand in hand with God as your foundation.

How can you and your spouse fight spiritual forces of wickedness together?

PRAYER IS CENTRAL

Continue earnestly in prayer, being vigilant in it with thanksgiving.

COLOSSIANS 4:2 NKJV

Through prayer, we admit our dependence on our heavenly Father. Through prayer, we call for him to work in our lives. Through prayer, we express trust that he will answer our cries and fulfill our needs according to his will. Without prayer we flaunt independence from him and demonstrate a self-sufficient attitude that dishonors his name and invites trouble and temptation.

You are not wise enough to guard yourself or your spouse on all sides, but God is, and he's happy to do so. Be vigilant in your prayer life and remember all the things you can thank God for. Staying connected to him will keep your heart focused and keep the ways of the flesh at bay.

In what ways can you cultivate a more consistent prayer life?

TRUSTWORTHY

I want you to understand that the head of every man is Christ, the head of a wife is her husband, and the head of Christ is God.

1 Corinthians 11:3 ESV

Husbands have been placed in a unique role to lead their families, and they are expected to do so with the kind of love and care Christ demonstrated. A man's position at the head of his family is not authoritative or drenched in displays of power. A godly man leads his family with strength that is displayed in humility, meekness, and sacrificial love. Christ's love and leadership were not harsh or prideful, and a husband's love and leadership shouldn't be either.

God has given you and your spouse unique roles. Peace is found by embracing his order and exemplifying his character within your given role. You have the privilege of serving each other in different ways and encouraging each other to honor the Lord in all you do. Remember that your response to God's instructions is an act of worship.

How can you and your spouse embrace God's instructions in 1 Corinthians?

OUR COMFORTER

Let your steadfast love comfort me
according to your promise to your servant.

PSALM 119:76 ESV

God promises to be there for us and offer us comfort whenever we need it. There are days when we may feel completely defeated, and there are days when difficult situations challenge our sense of comfort and security in God. On such days, we can rely on God's promise of love and comfort and know the Holy Spirit is there whether we feel him or not.

Problems come and go, but God's love and comfort are constant. It never changes or fades. His love can breathe new life into your marriage, job, ministry, or whatever else you need encouragement for. On hard days, soak in God's refreshing comfort that offers direction and purpose.

What challenges threaten the peace in your marriage, and how can you intentionally seek rest in God?

TOWARD THE GOAL

Brothers and sisters, I do not regard myself as having taken hold of it yet; but one thing I do: forgetting what lies behind and reaching forward to what lies ahead, I press on toward the goal for the prize of the upward call of God in Christ Jesus.

PHILIPPIANS 3:13-14 NASB

Christ's call on our lives lifts us up when distractions and frustrations threaten to derail us. When temptation looms, let's keep our eyes on the prize and remember how immeasurably more gratifying it is to follow Jesus than to go our own way. As we run forward after the Lord, he is with us every step of the way.

God does not want you to be haunted or overwhelmed by past or current sins. He calls you to keep your eyes on him and let go of the idea of perfection. He doesn't expect you to have everything figured out. He calls you to confess, accept his forgiveness, repent, and continue on the path he has for you.

How can you apply God's call to forward living to your marriage?

TIME MARCHES ON

Do not forget this one thing, dear friends: With the Lord a day is like a thousand years, and a thousand years are like a day.

2 PETER 3:8 NIV

God will rule the earth with perfect justice when the time is right. Although the chaos of the world makes it seem like he is taking too long, it's important to remember that his timing is different than ours. He knows exactly when to intervene, and we are called to trust him while we wait.

Pride will tell you to take matters into your own hands. Pride will tell you that it's your job to judge the wrongs of others, and that you know exactly how things should work out. Wisdom leaves judgment in God's hands. Humbly remember that God is in control, and none of us can fathom how he will intertwine all the details of history. He alone is sovereign and worthy of all praise.

How can you and your spouse encourage each other to be patient about God's timing?

OCTOBER 9

Let your wife be a fountain of blessing for you.
Rejoice in the wife of your youth.

Proverbs 5:18 NLT

Husbands and wives should pursue each other and find ways to bless one another throughout the duration of their marriage. We are meant to be captivated by each other. The world will tell you to feed your desires however you want, but Scripture offers another way.

Proverbs 5 is both encouraging and cautionary. It's a reminder to find great delight in your partner. It's cautionary because it's clear that you are meant to find delight in them alone. It's not right for your eyes to stray or your affections to be casually shared. Your devotion to your spouse will result in greater intimacy and satisfaction for both of you.

What are some specific ways you can pursue your spouse today?

MEDITATE AND LEARN

Keep this Book of the Law always on your lips; meditate on it day and night, so that you may be careful to do everything written in it. Then you will be prosperous and successful.

JOSHUA 1:8 NIV

It's easy to take Scripture for granted in our culture. We have unlimited access to it, and we are inundated with translations, commentaries, and interpretations. We don't have the context for what it might be like to live without it. As a result, we might not prioritize it like we should. We don't memorize Scripture because we can just pull out our phones and read it whenever we want.

Do you want your marriage to be prosperous? Scripture should play a big role. Do you want your life to be a success? Apply biblical truth to everything you do, and you will prosper. Fight against the urge to take the Word for granted. Take advantage of your unhindered access and store as much of it in your heart as you can.

What are some practical ways to keep Scripture always on our lips?

PEACEFUL ATMOSPHERE

A person's insight gives him patience, and his virtue is to overlook an offense.

PROVERBS 19:11 CSB

Wisdom and patience go hand in hand. In our current culture, the unangered, unperturbed person is rarely heralded as a source of truth. We look to loud showboats instead of patient role models. We tend to follow the most passionate or persuasive voice. Scripture teaches that there is far more value in having a quiet spirit.

Today's verse in invaluable in cultivating a healthy marriage. Being patient and slow to anger will always be the best path. You will never regret practicing those virtues. Both of those things lead to trust, security, and intimacy in relationships. A home that is defined by forgiveness and quiet patience is a home that allows people to feel safe to be themselves.

How can you practice patience and forgiveness with your spouse?

CLEAN HEART

If we confess our sins, he is faithful and just to forgive us our sins and to cleanse us from all unrighteousness.

1 JOHN 1:9 ESV

God is always true to his character, and he never goes back on his word. He sent his son to die, and he resurrected him from the grave so that we could be free. He made a way for us to enjoy the perfection of his presence for all eternity. After orchestrating all of history to secure our salvation, he won't go back on his promises now.

Look at what God has done for you! He has moved heaven and earth to call you his own. He didn't do all of that for you to remain in captivity. He longs for you to be free! He longs for you to approach him with confidence. He has done all the work needed. All you need to do is confess your sins and trust that he will keep his promises.

Is there an area of your life or marriage where you have let shame drive?

FORGIVENESS

Though he fall, he shall not be cast headlong, for the LORD upholds his hand.

PSALM 37:24 ESV

We cannot make a mistake so terrible that the Lord would not catch us. There are sins so offensive that we, as humans, struggle to forgive each other, but the Lord's forgiveness is always available to anyone who asks with a contrite heart.

When your spouse hurts you, it may be difficult to pardon them and not hold a grudge. It might not be easy, but it is possible because of the great love and forgiveness you have been shown. How can you hold a debt against someone when your debt has been wiped out completely? Remember that your spouse's sins are no greater or worse than your own, and God will give you grace to forgive them when it's beyond your ability.

Are you holding your spouse's sins when you could be forgiving them and letting go?

RACE TO WIN

Do you not know that in a race all the runners run, but only one gets the prize? Run in such a way as to get the prize.

1 CORINTHIANS 9:24 NIV

Our end goal should impact the way we run. In other words, if we want eternal life with Christ, we should act like it. We aren't meant to claim salvation as our own while stubbornly keeping our lives in our own hands. Our declaration of faith should result in the continuous transformation of our hearts and lives.

Are you racing with your eyes on the prize of Christ Jesus? Is your life focused and are your efforts intentional? Keep your eyes on Jesus, and you'll never miss a step. He has given you everything you need to run well. He doesn't expect you to muster up your own strength or rely on your own abilities. His grace is sufficient for every single step you take.

What does it look like to run well in this season of life? What does it look like for your spouse?

YOU MATTER

"The Lord your God in your midst,
The Mighty One, will save;
He will rejoice over you with gladness,
He will quiet you with His love,
He will rejoice over you with singing."

Zephaniah 3:17 NKJV

God rejoices over his children with gladness. He is happy to call us his own, and he is delighted by who we are. He is filled with affection for us, and he longs to be near us. He is not disappointed, angry, or frustrated with our failures. God is a kind, attentive, and thoughtful Father who is pleased with his children.

How do you feel about God rejoicing over you? Does his kindness throw you off or make you uncomfortable? Is it easier for you to imagine that he is stern, impatient, or aloof? Turn toward him and offer him your heart. Allow him to prove your perceptions wrong and enjoy the peace that comes from knowing you matter to him.

How does knowing you matter to God impact the way you love others including your spouse?

HOPEFUL FUTURE

She laughs without fear of the future.

PROVERBS 31:25 NLT

There is a common message being shared that everything is getting worse. We are constantly reminded that things aren't as good as they used to be. We are told that the outlook is grim socially, politically, and economically. It's difficult to imagine looking at the future with such carefree hope that we laugh about it. That reaction seems unrealistic and naïve.

Laughing at the future is only naïve if you don't know the end of the story. Thankfully, as a believer, you know full well that there is nothing to fear. God is sovereign and trustworthy. There is no political situation that stresses him out. There is no economic collapse that can hinder his plans. There is no social trend that can derail his purposes. You and your household can laugh at the days to come because God is in control, and he will keep his promises.

How can you and your spouse create a home that isn't afraid of the future?

KEEP THE FAITH

I have fought the good fight, I have finished the race, I have kept the faith.

2 Timothy 4:7 NKJV

Our titles don't matter as much as we might think they do. A CEO can be just as faithful to God as a janitor. A teacher can be just as faithful to God as someone who is unemployed. We tend to be overly concerned with our roles and successes, but God is much more concerned with the state of our hearts.

Consider the roles God has assigned you. You might not be exactly where you want to be, but what has God placed in your path right now? Seek to honor him in your present condition. Surrender your plans to him and give him your heart. Perseverance and strength of faith matter so much more than the details of your life.

How can you and your spouse honor God with faithfulness and humility in your current roles?

GOD'S PREPARATIONS

"No eye has seen, no ear has heard, and no mind has imagined what God has prepared for those who love him."

1 CORINTHIANS 2:9 NLT

When we think about the future, our minds constantly play out different scenarios and possibilities, but God's plans are better than we can imagine. We can't know for sure what each of our days will look like, but we can look toward eternity with a great amount of confidence. We can be assured that he has wonderful things in store for us.

Your future is less uncertain than you might think. Perhaps you're stuck in a dead-end job, floating between houses, or pushing through the daily grind with no end in sight. Whatever the case, your path is not random or hopeless. If you are following the Lord, you are moving toward eternal life. God will be faithful to you no matter what your circumstances look like along the way.

How can you maintain faith when you are discouraged by your circumstances?

Let brotherly love continue. Do not forget to entertain strangers, for by so doing some have unwittingly entertained angels.

HEBREWS 13:1-2 NKJV

Today's Scripture encourages us to be hospitable. It reminds us that we won't always know the impact of our kindness. Our small offerings might change someone's life. The way we love others has ripple effects that can be seen through generations.

You and your spouse have the opportunity to be generous with what you have. Open your home despite your insecurities or discomfort. It doesn't matter if you think you don't have anything worth sharing. It also doesn't matter if you'd rather keep your earthly treasures to yourself. Choose generosity no matter which end of the spectrum you are on. Let your open-handed kindness be an act of worship to the Lord who deserves everything you have.

How can you and your spouse be generous with whatever you've been given?

ACCOUNTABLE TO GOD

Do not let any part of your body become an instrument of evil to serve sin. Instead, give yourselves completely to God, for you were dead, but now you have new life. So use your whole body as an instrument to do what is right for the glory of God.

ROMANS 6:13 NLT

In Christ, we have the understanding we need to commit our bodies to acts of righteousness. We do this to honor the Lord who created us. We offer him our lives because he laid his down so willingly. Loyalty to our spouse is a biproduct of our obedience to God.

You won't be successful in your fight against sin if your spouse is your highest level of accountability. You cannot live to please another fallible human. Strength to stand firm against evil can only come from the Lord. He is the only one who can take your feeble offerings and give you grace to remain faithful.

Are there areas of your life in which you've held your spouse's preferences above the Lord's?

LIFE ADVENTURES

How blessed is the person whose strength is in You,
In whose heart are the roads to Zion!

PSALM 84:5 NASB

Zion, or Jerusalem, was where the temple of God stood. People were so desperate to be in the presence of the Almighty they were willing to travel the long highway to get there. Having the highways to Zion in our hearts is symbolic of someone who is willing to go as far as it takes to be close to God.

God promises blessings for a life of devotion. He encourages you to find your strength in him instead of your own abilities or talents. He knows that the path he asks you to follow isn't always easy, but he also promises to give you everything you need to stay on it. When you give him your life, he never leaves your side.

How can you and your spouse seek the Lord fervently together?

STORMY WATERS

We also glory in our sufferings, because we know that suffering produces perseverance; perseverance, character; and character, hope.

ROMANS 5:3-4 NIV

Belonging to Christ does not mean we are exempt from enduring difficulties. Unlike everyone else, however, our sufferings provide us with a benefit. We know that every trial we walk through strengthens us. Difficult days are not meaningless or without purpose. Our suffering is never wasted.

The sorrows and trials you face as a married couple can grow your love rather than diminish it. They can produce perseverance, and they can make you more resilient. You become stronger when you trust God to work through your most difficult days. Put your hardships in his hands, and he will use them for his glory and your good.

What stormy waters have led to the hope you now have in God's promises?

RELATIONAL EQUITY

Let us not neglect our meeting together, as some people do, but encourage one another, especially now that the day of his return is drawing near.

HEBREWS 10:25 NLT

Marriage requires intentionality even in good times. If we wait until hardships happen or our failures rise to the surface, we won't be equipped to stand strong. We can use seasons of normalcy to develop healthy habits, so we are prepared when life doesn't feel quite so easy.

Trials will reveal the patterns you've invested in. You can't always control which hardships you'll face, but you can control how much relational equity you have. If you've spent time cultivating healthy dynamics like encouraging each other or thoughtfully building intimacy, you will reap the benefits in difficult seasons. When trials take a large withdrawal from your relationship, you won't be left with a zero balance.

What can you do today to build up equity in your relationship?

BROKEN PROMISES

If we are faithless, He remains faithful, for He cannot deny Himself.

2 TIMOTHY 2:13 NASB

God knew we would break our promises before he made a covenant with us. He knew that we would not be capable of staying the course on our own. Our weaknesses and inevitable sin did not deter him. He chose to be faithful knowing that we would be unfaithful.

Remember this aspect of God's character when your spouse lets you down. Sometimes you might feel the urge to even the score or drop your end of the bargain. Thankfully, that's not God's response when you miss the mark. When you are disappointed, stay faithful. With God's help you can be constant, reliable, loyal, and encouraging.

When your spouse falls short, how can you respond in a way that reflects God's faithfulness?

ENRICH EACH OTHER

Her husband can trust her, and she will greatly enrich his life. She brings him good, not harm, all the days of her life.

PROVERBS 31:11-12 NLT

Marriage is an invitation to consistently enrich the life of another person. We aren't meant to enter into marriage for the ways we will benefit. The heart of the marriage commitment is sacrifice, selflessness, and the good of the other. We choose to remain loyal, faithful, and trustworthy out of love for the person we've vowed to be with for all our days.

How are you enriching the life of your spouse? If your answer doesn't ever change, it might be time for some creativity. Look beyond the first things that come to mind. There is always room to grow when it comes to thoughtfully and sacrificially loving your spouse. Each day you have the opportunity to love each other in a way that feels like the gift of a lifetime.

What's something different you can do to enrich each other's lives today?

ALLEGIANCE

Let us offer through Jesus a continual sacrifice of praise to God, proclaiming our allegiance to his name.

HEBREWS 13:15 NLT

Allegiance can be described as loyalty, commitment, fidelity, duty, and faithfulness. Jesus Christ was so committed to us that he reconciled our disloyalty to him by laying down his own life. He willingly suffered under the weight of our sin, and he asks for our faithfulness in return.

What can you offer as thanks for his incredible gift? You get to praise his name, offer him your allegiance, and be loyal in your marriage. To dutifully stick to those things, it's important to seek him daily and rely on his strength. Praise God for his loyal commitment to you and follow his example in your commitments to others.

How can you and your spouse reassure each other of your loyalty?

UNDERSTANDING

As the heavens are higher than the earth, so are my ways higher than your ways, and my thoughts than your thoughts.

Isaiah 55:9 NKJV

It is tempting to take our lives into our own hands. We often think we know best. We assume that our plans and ideas are good and that we know what our lives should look like. We cross into dangerous waters when we begin to believe that our limited perception is as vast as God's. As his children, we should be wary of assuming that we are anything but short-sighted.

It takes humility to follow the Lord. Acknowledging the frailty of your humanity is necessary in order to be submissive to his ways. His thoughts and plans are so much better than you could ever imagine, but you won't experience them if you're convinced that you know best. Quiet your heart, seek lowliness, and put your days into his capable hands.

Have you and your spouse created a plan for your future? Are you constantly submitting it to God and staying poised to receive his revisions?

VALUE

Who can find a virtuous wife?
For her worth is far above rubies.

PROVERBS 31:10 NKJV

There are several places in the Scriptures that prize virtue and wisdom above the value of precious stones and great wealth. One of those places is the depiction of the famous Proverbs 31 woman. She has great wisdom, is industrious, and cares so deeply for her family that Solomon claims a wife like this is more valuable than rubies.

God is not impressed with the glittering riches that catch your eye. He is not swayed by external beauty or momentary success. You can follow his example by refusing to be enraptured by the beauty of the world. Remember that the most attractive things about your spouse are the ways in which their character reflects the Lord. Cultivate virtue within your marriage, and you won't be disappointed.

How can you encourage the virtues you see in your spouse?

ALL IN

"If you refuse to take up your cross and follow me, you are not worthy of being mine. If you cling to your life, you will lose it; but if you give up your life for me, you will find it."

MATTHEW 10:38-39 NLT

Commitment requires sacrifice. We can't choose to follow Jesus and refuse to do anything about it. We can't say that we are faithful to him but remain unwilling to follow his ways or listen to his instructions. Similarly, we shouldn't say marriage vows without the intent to lay down our lives and love each other selflessly.

Your marriage requires effort. In fact, it requires more effort than any other relationship you have. The good news is that your diligence does not go unrewarded. You will reap what you sow when it comes to your marriage. There might be seasons of heartache or pain, but there can also be seasons of intense joy and satisfaction. Follow up your vows with intentional commitment, and you will reap the benefits.

Are there areas of your marriage that you haven't invested in for a while?

WELL ARMORED

Put on every piece of God's armor so you will be able to resist the enemy in the time of evil. Then after the battle you will still be standing firm.

EPHESIANS 6:13 NLT

It is easy to feel overwhelmed, angry, or scared when you look at the state of the world. There are so many confused voices shouting misguided ideologies and contradictory information. We are pushed to pick a side, care only about ourselves, and embrace whatever is fed to us. When we steal away from the world and find a quiet moment to soak in the Word of God, we remember again that we are never alone.

God goes before you, and he never leaves your side. He is not surprised by the state of things, and he will never leave you defenseless. He is constantly equipping you for the battles you will face. He knows exactly what you need, and he won't let you down. When the world is overwhelming, look to him and remember that he promises to stay with you.

What can you and your spouse do to face the world with confidence and quiet hearts?

PRICE OF WEALTH

Better is the little of the righteous
Than the abundance of many wicked.

PSALM 37:16 NASB

The abundance of the wicked may seem tantalizing to those of us who have very little, but meager wages earned honestly are more valuable than dishonest riches. To gain wealth through evil means is worthless because the days of the wicked are numbered. We are instructed to offer what we have to God and find contentment in his love.

This life and its treasures will all fade away one day, so it would be foolish to trade your soul for comfortable living here and now. All the pleasures of this life pale in comparison to a life lived serving him; for true joy can only be found in him. He is the source of both your purpose and pleasure.

What do you and your spouse have that can be used to serve God?

NOVEMBER

Love does not demand its own way.
It is not irritable, and it keeps no record
of being wronged.

1 Corinthians 13:5 NLT

LOVING CORRECTION

He who heeds discipline shows the way to life,
but whoever ignores correction leads others astray.

PROVERBS 10:17 NIV

The Lord disciplines those he loves because he cares about our development and our maturity. If we are humble enough to receive his loving discipline and grow from it, we can use his lessons, and the wisdom they have taught us, to bless others.

When you live contrary to God's ordinances and are unwilling to learn or yield, it is to your detriment and the detriment of others. You can be a blessing or a hinderance to your spouse, family, and friends. Keep other people in mind when you are choosing which course to take.

How do you and your spouse respond to correction?

THE GREATEST SACRIFICE

"God so loved the world that he gave his one and only Son, that whoever believes in him shall not perish but have eternal life."

JOHN 3:16 NIV

God's love for us is exemplified by sacrifice. Jesus' life, death, and resurrection was perfect display of how much God cares for us. He spared no expense in making a way for us to be with him forever.

If you want the love within your marriage to reflect God, it must also be exemplified by sacrifice. This means you will need to give up what you want in favor of your husband or wife. This sounds like a romantic idea but the practicalities of it can be more difficult. Sacrifice is often messy and inconvenient. It can happen in simple ways like keeping quiet when you don't really like dinner, or it can happen in big ways like responding graciously when your husband or wife makes a grievous mistake.

When has your spouse chosen to love you sacrificially? When have you done the same?

GIVE HONOR

You husbands must give honor to your wives. Treat your wife with understanding as you live together. She may be weaker than you are, but she is your equal partner in God's gift of new life. Treat her as you should so your prayers will not be hindered.

1 Peter 3:7 NLT

What does it mean to treat someone with understanding? The first step is taking the time to know the details of their situation. We won't treat others rightly if we don't know their strengths, weaknesses, or circumstances. Adjusting our behavior based on the knowledge we have shows humility and maturity.

A godly husband takes the time to understand his wife. He is thoughtful toward her, and he knows what she needs. He praises her strengths, and he takes her weaknesses into account. He offers her protection over judgment, kindness over criticism, and selflessness over pride. He doesn't diminish her, but he highly esteems her.

How can you and your spouse honor God's idea of treating each other with understanding?

SUBMIT IN LOVE

Submit to one another out of reverence for Christ.

EPHESIANS 5:21 NIV

Submission does not involve passively following what someone else says or does. Submission involves putting the needs of others above our own. We can do this because of our reverence for Christ and because we see how he put our needs before his own wellbeing.

Within the bond of marriage, the Bible is clear that we are to submit to each other and put the needs of our spouses above our own. This provides a clear picture of Christ's love to anyone privy to the union, and it also creates harmony and safety for both husband and wife.

How can you choose to put your spouse first today?

BLESSED BY TRUST

His pleasure is not in the strength of the horse,
nor his delight in the legs of the warrior;
the LORD delights in those who fear him,
who put their hope in his unfailing love.

PSALM 147:10-11 NIV

Our demonstrations of power and might do not impress the Lord. He wants us to learn how to trust in him and rely on his strength, rather than attempt to muscle our way through life by our own means and willpower. Humility is far more pleasing to the Lord than ability. Our skills and strength are gifts from him, and humble love is our grateful gift back to him.

God holds all the power in the universe, and yet also holds you gently in his embrace. He offers you leadership and guidance that is so much better than your own skills or abilities. Following his ways and putting your hope in his love is always the best path. You will be blessed by trusting in the Lord above all else.

What are some practical ways you and your spouse can lean on God's strength before your own?

IF YOU LOVE ME

"If you love Me, keep My commandments."

JOHN 14:15 NKJV

A life that is devoted to Jesus will have proof. We can't say we are his followers without actually following his instructions. We adjust the way we think, speak, and behave because we know that his ways are best. We allow him to transform our hearts and lives because we know that he is worth every ounce of sacrifice.

In the same way, your life should bear the fruit of being devoted to your spouse. You can't say marriage vows and then refuse to put them into practice. Your life should be filled with daily evidence that you love your husband or wife. You won't get it right all the time, but humility, consistency, and perseverance go a long way. Set your standards high and seek to love well each day.

How can you practically fulfill your marriage vows today?

PERSISTENCE IN PRAYER

The Lord hears his people
when they call to him for help.
He rescues them from all their troubles.

Psalm 34:17 NLT

It's easy to give up on prayer when we don't experience results in the time we anticipated. As children of God, we need never feel hopeless because help will always come. The journey may not be the easiest or most comfortable. God may seem silent or the path unbearable, but if we pray to God, he most definitely hears and will always deliver his children.

What troubles are you facing today? Have you been praying about them for a long time? Don't give up! The Lord hears you, and he will certainly rescue you from all your troubles. Cling to Scripture when you are discouraged. Partner with your spouse in believing for the best and keep trusting in God's strength over your own.

How can you and your spouse support each other in persistent prayer?

INTIMATE

His left hand is under my head,
And his right hand embraces me.

SONG OF SOLOMON 8:3 NKJV

There is a love, pure and intimate, that cares genuinely for another person. Picture two lovers: his arm is under her head because they are facing each other. Their focus is on each other. He embraces her because they are comfortable and close together. The love they share isn't self-seeking; its interest and concern is for the other person.

This is the kind of love God wants us to experience with each other. Our marriages can be intimate, comfortable, and focused on one another because that is the love Christ gives us and teaches us to give to each other. If we take the time to cultivate trust, the result is safety, intimacy, and comfortable love.

What can you do this week to cultivate deeper love and intimacy?

HEART AT REST

The Lord will be your confidence
and will keep your foot from a snare.

Proverbs 3:26 CSB

We do not live as the rest of the world lives. When crisis hits, we remain unshaken because our confidence comes from God. We don't rely on our own strength, the abilities of others, or the systems of the world. We don't find security in the government, comfortable circumstances, or the absence of suffering. We trust in God and believe that he holds everything in his hands. He is the reason we aren't afraid of falling.

God is your assurance and firm foundation. No catastrophe or crippling condition can cause you to lose heart when it is God who holds you together. You can trust him to guide you and keep you safe. He is more than just a King; he is also an involved and loving Father who covers you with his peace and fills you with confidence.

In the midst of crisis, what truths can you remind yourself of?

EXPANSIVE LOVE

Your love, Lord, reaches to the heavens,
your faithfulness to the skies.
Your righteousness is like the highest mountains,
your justice like the great deep.
You, Lord, preserve both people and animals.

Psalm 36:5-6 NIV

God is great and glorious. Just as heaven is infinite, God's attributes are infinite in their magnitude. Our love is a drop in the bucket compared to the ocean of God's love. Even an ocean is too small to portray the depth and breadth of God's affection for us.

God's love sustains you. He preserves your life, and he keeps you safe. He faithfully watches over you, and he provides for your needs. His heart is inclined toward you, and he cares for you. His love and commitment goes far beyond anything you can understand.

How does being assured of God's great love impact your daily life?

STAND STRONG

Rejoice in hope,
be patient in tribulation,
be constant in prayer.

ROMANS 12:12 ESV

We should expect life to push against us. We are children of the King living in enemy territory. The devil does not want us to flourish in our faith; he wants to crush us. Once we get past the idea that this world should be easier, we find the truth of God's plan for our lives.

God has equipped you to withstand the trials of this life. He has given you everything you need to stay steady when your circumstances are stormy. He has not abandoned you, and he never will. If life feels impossible, remember that God is with you. He reminds you to rejoice, be patient, and call upon his name anytime.

If you have let the trials of life bring you down, how can you come back into alignment with God's plans?

STRENGTH AND COURAGE

"Be strong and do not lose courage, for there is a reward for your work."

2 CHRONICLES 15:7 NASB

The strong and courageous are those who seek God when they wake up, serve their families, are faithful to their spouses, and share generously with those who need it. The strong and courageous are those who will not be deterred by trivial tasks, petty issues, or the bad behavior of those around them. The strong and courageous are those who sacrifice comfort for eternal rewards and care for the needs of others even if those they serve can never return the favor.

God defines strength and courage differently than the world does. His kingdom is not built on the same principles as the systems of the world. He knows that it isn't easy to go against the grain, but he gives you everything you need to live rightly. He equips you, and he promises to reward you.

Do your life and marriage reflect the ways of the world or the ways of God's kingdom?

TRUSTING TOGETHER

Those who know the LORD trust him,
because he will not leave those who come to him.

PSALM 9:10 NCV

We sometimes struggle to trust the Lord. He has been faithful, and we have experienced his goodness, yet we are tempted by the world and our weaknesses easily expose our humanity. We are quick to forget his good works, and we become discouraged by the trials we face. The solution to our wavering trust is to get to know God.

When you know someone well, you have a clear picture of their character. When you know their character, you have a good idea of how they will react in various situations. If you believe your spouse is loyal, you won't be swayed by the opinions of people who don't matter. In the same way, if you believe God wants to help you, you won't be discouraged when his timing is different from what you expect.

How do you encourage your spouse to continue trusting the Lord?

WINNING

We do not lose heart. Though outwardly we are wasting away, yet inwardly we are being renewed day by day. For our light and momentary troubles are achieving for us an eternal glory that far outweighs them all.

2 Corinthians 4:16-17 NIV

Life can be difficult, and our paths aren't always smooth, but the Bible promises that even though our bodies waste away, God is renewing us every day. He gives us fresh strength, new hope, refined wisdom, and a deeper knowledge of him. The glory to come outshines any suffering or hardship we're currently facing.

Keep pressing on, don't lose heart, and hold on to your faith. It will only get better with time. Even when it looks like you are losing, you are always winning with God. What a glorious promise! Remember that your perception isn't always accurate, and you can trust God with the bigger picture of your life.

How has God gotten you and your spouse through difficult seasons in the past?

THE LORD'S DIRECTION

May the Lord direct your hearts into the love of God and into the patience of Christ.

2 Thessalonians 3:5 NKJV

We can't bring anything to God without his help. He loved us first, and everything we do is a response to him. He created us, called us his own, and he continues to sustain our relationship with him. By his grace, we turn our hearts toward him and follow his example. Every interaction we have with him sits on the foundation of his faithfulness rather than our own.

Your relationship with God is built upon the strength of his character. Your relationships with other people are meant to be the same. When your commitment to your spouse is founded upon the Lord's unending faithfulness, it will stand the test of time. If it is built on your own ability to endure, it may not last. You are stronger together when your eyes on him.

How does depending on God's strength make your marriage stronger?

GIVING CHEERFULLY

> *You must each decide in your heart how much to give. And don't give reluctantly or in response to pressure. "For God loves a person who gives cheerfully."*
>
> 2 Corinthians 9:7 NLT

God is not lacking in resources; he has all the power and wealth in the universe. It is our honor to be able to give back to him what he has entrusted to us. When we are generous with our finances, we declare that money is not where we find our security. When we choose to keep our hands open and our resources available to others, we show that we are willing to trust the Lord with our circumstances.

There is so much joy to be found in being cheerful givers. Together you and your spouse have the opportunity to reflect God's generosity to the people around you. You can give freely from your finances, time, or energy. You can show up when people need help and enjoy the satisfaction of living for something other than your own comfort.

How can you and your spouse grow in generosity?

GOOD THOUGHTS

I remember the days of old;
I meditate on all that you have done;
I ponder the work of your hands.

PSALM 143:5 ESV

Joy is found in deliberately remembering the goodness of God. Our current circumstances might not be ideal, but we can't deny that God has moved on our behalf countless times before. He has done great things for those who love him and follow his ways. When we choose to recount his faithfulness, we strengthen ourselves for future trials.

Sit down with your spouse and talk about God's faithfulness. Remind each other of the work of his hands and be encouraged by where the conversation leads you. Take a break from focusing on your immediate problems and find hope in the ways God has already shown up. Turn your collective gaze toward God's proven goodness.

In what ways has God already shown up for you and your spouse?

VULNERABLE LOVE

Whoever isolates himself seeks his own desire;
he breaks out against all sound judgment.

PROVERBS 18:1 ESV

It's possible to be surrounded by people and be fully isolated. Isolation is not necessarily a physical problem. We isolate ourselves when we refuse to be honest, vulnerable, and authentic with the people in our lives. Holding back is detrimental to us, and we rob the people around us of intimacy and connection.

It takes courage to offer your heart to someone. It takes humility to cultivate real connection because it means allowing others to see your flaws and downfalls. It might seem more comfortable to offer the world a curated version of yourself, but that's not best for anyone. Choose to live boldly in the light and enjoy the shared wisdom and love of authentic connection.

Are there areas of your marriage where you can increase vulnerability?

ACCEPTABLE WORDS

Let the words of my mouth
and the meditation of my heart
be acceptable to you,
O Lord, my rock and my redeemer.

Psalm 19:14 ESV

Scripture is clear that our words matter. God outlines numerous ways in which we can reflect his character with what we say. We know that we are supposed to speak the truth in love, edify others, and continually praise God. The execution of this is where we sometimes get tangled up. This is why Psalm 19 is so encouraging. It reminds us that we can ask God for help in this area.

Offer your words to the Lord. Invite him to help you control your tongue. Tell him that you want him to be honored not only by what you say but by what's inside your heart. As you continually surrender in this way, you make room for his Spirit to teach and guide you. Don't be dismayed by your own inability but be encouraged by God's willingness to help you.

Does the way you and your spouse speak to each other honor the Lord?

THOUGHT LIFE

Whatever is true, whatever is honorable, whatever is right, whatever is pure, whatever is lovely, whatever is commendable, if there is any excellence and if anything worthy of praise, think about these things.

PHILIPPIANS 4:8 NASB

The mind is the starting point for behavior. When the evil one wants to entice a person to sin, he starts in their mind. He speaks lies and condemnation until he gets the emotional response he is looking for. When anxious thoughts flood our minds or we are tempted to sin, our immediate reaction should be to look to Jesus and remember who we are in Christ.

You are the only one who is responsible for your thoughts. If Scripture encourages you to think about what is true, honorable, and right, then you can trust that you are capable of controlling what you think. You get to decide what occupies your mind and how it impacts your life. Your thoughts matter, and God encourages you to be mindful of them.

What is the best way for you and your spouse to hold each other accountable to honorable thoughts?

CONTENTMENT

I know what it is to be in need, and I know what it is to have plenty. I have learned the secret of being content in any and every situation, whether well fed or hungry, whether living in plenty or in want.

PHILIPPIANS 4:12 NIV

The world constantly tells us what we need. The popular message is that our happiness is based on what we have and what we've achieved. We are subtly told that our current circumstances aren't good enough and that happiness will come with just one more purchase. As believers, we know that this isn't the case. We know that true contentment doesn't come from external circumstances.

Imagine what your home might feel like if you and your spouse were truly content. Imagine the peace you might feel without that nagging feeling that you constantly need something more or different to be happy. Let God's Word be rooted in your heart and accept his offer to find true satisfaction in his presence.

Are there specific things you and your spouse have attached the idea of happiness to?

BE STILL

"The Lord will fight for you;
you need only to be still."

Exodus 14:14 NIV

God's timing is not our timing, and we often become impatient and attempt to take matters into our own hands. The Bible is full of individuals who tried to force God's hand or rush his plan. It's hard to drop an offense or move past a wrongdoing without trying to enact our own imperfect version of justice.

Your sight is limited, but God sees the big picture. He knows what the entire battle looks like. This is why he asks you to let him fight for you. You might have your own best interests in mind, but he has everyone's best interests in mind simultaneously. He is the only one who can weave the details together perfectly. Surrendering to him is a declaration that he is capable, strong, and wise.

Are there battles within your marriage that you've taken control of instead of surrendering them to God?

GOOD WORK

Let us not become weary in doing good, for at the proper time we will reap a harvest if we do not give up.

GALATIANS 6:9 NIV

Today's Scripture is incredibly validating. The admonition to stay strong indicates that we won't always feel like it. God knows full well that we will get tired of doing the right thing. He encourages us to keep going because he knows that the reward is worth the pain. Our weariness is normal, but we must still handle it the right way.

Marriage is rarely fair. There are very few seasons where the responsibilities and burdens are perfectly divided. There will be times when you pick up the slack for your spouse and times when they do the same for you. When it's your turn, don't become weary. Recognize that you are tired but allow the Lord to strengthen you. Acknowledge your weariness and also acknowledge that doing what's right is better than quitting.

How can you and your spouse encourage each other through weariness?

OLIVE BRANCH

How good and pleasant it is
when God's people live together in unity!

Psalm 133:1 NIV

It takes effort to maintain unity, but the work is far outvalued by the reward. It's beautiful and pleasant when God's people live together in unity. We glorify him when we compensate for each other's weaknesses and celebrate each other's strength. We honor him when we offer to help those who are weak and when we refuse to let petty differences cause dissension.

Unity within marriage is not elusive, and there are practical ways to achieve it. Talk about your goals and values. Decide what is most important to you as a team and strive to stay focused on it. Be aware the things that cause frustration between the two of you, and don't sacrifice peace for the momentary satisfaction of being right. Protect each other's weaknesses and remember that you are a team.

What actions can you take to fight for unity in your marriage, in your community, and in your country?

RESTORATION

When they had finished breakfast, Jesus said to Simon Peter, "Simon, son of John, do you love me more than these?" He said to him, "Yes, Lord; you know that I love you." He said to him, "Feed my lambs."

JOHN 21:15 ESV

There is much to glean from this encounter between Jesus and Peter. Peter had messed up. In his Lord's most difficult moments, Peter abandoned him. It was a terrible betrayal, but it was not a surprise to Jesus. He knew Peter would let him down, yet he chose to call him anyway.

Like Peter, we let Jesus down all the time. We fail to measure up, but that doesn't come as a surprise to Jesus. He knew we would fail, but he chose to love us, save us, and help us anyway. Don't be deterred when you fail. Take Jesus' hand, get back up, and try again.

Are there areas of your marriage where you've let failure keep you from moving forward?

DEPENDENCY

The LORD protects those of childlike faith;
I was facing death, and he saved me.

PSALM 116:6 NLT

Our society is deeply individualistic. We encourage self-reliance, independence, and personal success. Our society is not community based, and a lot of people just want to be left alone. We don't want to be relied upon, and we look to have as little responsibility as possible.

Children are highly dependent, and God says this is wonderful. He encourages you to be like a child. He calls you to a life of trust and reliance on this strength. He asks you to shy away from the idea that you can do everything on your own. Instead of becoming more independent as you get older, God invites you to become more child-like.

How can you embrace child-like dependance in your marriage?

GLAD FOR TODAY

This is the day that the Lord has made;
let us rejoice and be glad in it.

Psalm 118:24 ESV

Every single day of our lives is an opportunity to rejoice and be glad. If God made it, it is good. He created time, with each day being a testimony to his goodness. Every morning when we wake up, we can praise God for the work of his hands. We can choose to be thankful for what he's done, or we can choose to ignore it.

It might sound cliché, but there is always a reason to be thankful. It really will transform the way you think if you deliberately look for reasons to be grateful. Even the smallest joys are worthy of praising God. In fact, being thankful for the seemingly insignificant parts of your day has the greatest power to generate radical change in your heart.

How can you commit this day, along with your heart and mind, to the Lord?

FAITHFULNESS

As for me, I shall sing of Your strength;
Yes, I shall joyfully sing of Your faithfulness
in the morning,
For You have been my refuge
And a place of refuge on the day of my distress.

PSALM 59:16 NASB

It takes discipline to remember the goodness of God. It's easy to become weighed down by the cares of life, and each of us has a number of burdens we can choose to carry. We all have pain and trials to endure. Instead of focusing on what's difficult, we can focus on God's faithfulness. We can remember that he is strong even when we are weak.

God is capable of carrying each of your burdens. He is faithful whether you are overwhelmed about money, struggling to communicate with your spouse, or dealing with significant trauma. His strength is enough for you, and he promises to be with you on the day of your distress.

What encourages you in the morning and prepares you for the day?

BEST CONSULTANT

Trust in the LORD with all your heart
And do not lean on your own understanding.

PROVERBS 3:5 NASB

The point of King Solomon's message was not to promote ignorance or discourage sound reasoning but to caution us that even the most intelligent person is fallible and subject to bias. Any of us can be misled because we do not have the full picture the way God does. We trust him because his track record is flawless. We declare that his ways are better than our own because he has proven himself time and time again.

Leaning on God is much safer than leaning on your own understanding. Think about how this might apply to your marriage. You cannot possibly see your spouse perfectly all the time, but God does. God sees both of your hearts clearly even when you feel frustrated, annoyed, or impatient. If you ask him, he will help you navigate your relationship with grace and kindness.

How can you lean on God's understanding in your marriage?

STRONGER TOGETHER

A person standing alone can be attacked and defeated, but two can stand back-to-back and conquer. Three are even better, for a triple-braided cord is not easily broken.

ECCLESIASTES 4:12 NLT

Four hands are better than two, and two heads can solve a problem quicker than one. We are meant to rely on each other. Each of us have unique and important strengths that we bring into marriage. When combined with our third partner, God, we become a powerful team equipped to deal with what life may throw our way.

One of the greatest things about marriage is that you have a teammate. Throughout your life, you have someone to watch out for your interests and have your back. Life is easier with a partner. You can rely on each other, encourage each other, and fight for each other when your strength is diminished. When you feel like you can't keep going, a companion makes all the difference.

How can you offer a greater sense of companionship to your spouse today?

DECEMBER

Above all, keep loving one another earnestly, since love covers a multitude of sins.

1 Peter 4:8 ESV

POSSIBLE

Looking at them, Jesus said, "With people it is impossible, but not with God; for all things are possible with God."

MARK 10:27 NASB

How often do we tell God our deepest desires? As children, we have no problem praying for a ballgame win or a new baby brother, but as adults, we tend to lose the art of entrusting our dreams to the Lord. Maybe we keep a mental list of the times he hasn't answered our prayers the way we wanted, or we might think he has better things to do. Either way, it's time to reawaken our inner child who longs to open up to the Lord and trust him in all things.

Boldly offer your wildest dreams to God. It's likely that he is the one who put that desire in your heart in the first place. Ask him how you can honor him with your hopes and dreams. Surrender your gifts and talents to him and give him leadership over your plans. Let him be the one to decide whether or not something is possible.

Do you and your partner have dreams that you've set aside?

MUNDANE MATTERS

I want you to understand what really matters, so that you may live pure and blameless lives until the day of Christ's return.

PHILIPPIANS 1:10 NLT

Most people struggle with the mundane tasks of everyday life. Do they really matter? What eternal weight do they carry? Wouldn't our precious time and effort be better spent on more important things? As holy as that sounds, God has given us simple tasks because they can teach us about him. God is patient and humble. He esteems the lowly, and he prioritizes servanthood.

Offer your mundane tasks to the Lord as an act of worship. Your day might be filled with balancing the budget, changing dirty diapers, heading to a mediocre job, washing dishes, or a variety of thankless tasks. Remember that Jesus also paid taxes, washed feet, worked as a carpenter, and lived a regular life. His fully human days were lived out for the eternal glory of the Father. Your small tasks matter, and God sees your faithful work.

How can you encourage each other to find meaning in the seemingly insignificant parts of life?

FIRST

We love, because He first loved us.

1 John 4:19 NKJV

A good relationship is not made of two people who each give fifty percent. A good relationship is made of two people who are willing to give their all when their partner gives nothing. We take turns carrying unfair burdens because we are committed to the health of the team rather than being focused on ourselves. Sometimes we carry more than our fair share, and sometimes we lean on our partners and let them carry us.

This is the precedent God set; he loved us before we loved him. A love like this is a true marker of commitment. It shows the other person that you are there for them even when they are at their worst. Your ability to love each other without keeping score shows that you have experienced the undeserved and faithful love of God.

In what ways can you love your spouse without expecting anything in return?

THE BEST PROMISE

"If I go and prepare a place for you, I will come back and take you to be with me that you also may be where I am."

JOHN 14:3 NIV

This world is not our ultimate destination, so we should consider the eternal value of our investments. How we spend our time, money, and energy matters. We do not exist for this life alone but for the hope of an eternal home with Jesus. Although our intention may be to live intentionally and offer praise to God while here on earth, it is easy to succumb to the temptations and distractions we are constantly inundated with.

It's healthy to regularly assess the state of your heart. Are you overwhelmed by the worries of this life, or are your eyes set upon the age to come? Are you infatuated with momentary comforts or are you persevering with eternal glory in mind? Your greatest treasures are not found here, but they are found in God's eternal kingdom.

How can you help remind your spouse of their true nature and calling?

COURAGE AND FAITH

We are not like those who turn away from God to their own destruction. We are the faithful ones, whose souls will be saved.

HEBREWS 10:39 NLT

The Lord wants us to courageously live like Christ in a world that doesn't respect him or his way of doing things. How we speak, act, and make decisions will be confusing to a population rooted in self-interest and temporary living. Even our marriages look different because they exist to serve him rather than ourselves.

It won't always be easy to swim against the current of this culture, but your faith in the Lord provides you the courage and assurance you need to stay strong and continue. Take the path less trodden, read his Word to light your way, and lean on your spouse when times get hard. Marriage provides a wonderful partnership to help you along the way.

How has your spouse helped you remain faithful in your relationship with God?

NORMALIZE HAPPINESS

"When a man has taken a new wife, he shall not go out to war or be charged with any business; he shall be free at home one year, and bring happiness to his wife whom he has taken."

DEUTERONOMY 24:5 NKJV

God gave the Israelites an incredible mandate! He takes marriage seriously, and he knows how important a solid foundation is. Although this Old Testament law is not as applicable in modern society, the principle behind it can still be respected.

It isn't selfish to invest in your marriage. Your time together is precious and worth being protected. Don't let anyone hassle you about spending time with your spouse. Prioritize making each other happy in a culture that normalizes speaking negatively about a nagging wife or a lazy husband. Cultivate a relationship that is mutually satisfying to each of you. Focus on each other and put in the time needed to build a strong foundation.

How does your spouse bring you happiness?

GOD'S SUPPLY

My God will supply all your needs according to His riches in glory in Christ Jesus.

PHILIPPIANS 4:19 NASB

God has riches beyond our wildest imagination. He lacks nothing, and he wants to share everything with us. He cares about needs that go beyond paying bills or meeting deadlines. He cares about the state of our hearts. He wants us to trust him in moments of physical need and in moments of spiritual, emotional, or mental need. His provision includes but isn't limited to the food on our table and the clothes on our back.

God cares about your needs. He is generous, and he is capable of providing for you. His provision might not look how you expect, but that doesn't mean he isn't faithful. He is so proud of you when you depend on him, and he is pleased when you call upon his name.

How can you develop an atmosphere of trust and dependence within your home?

GOOD SHEPHERD

The Lord is my shepherd; I shall not want.
He makes me lie down in green pastures.
He leads me beside still waters.
He restores my soul.
He leads me in paths of righteousness
for his name's sake.

Psalm 23:1-3 ESV

Without a shepherd, sheep are vulnerable to all the elements and dangers of the wild. Even finding food and water would be a struggle without a kind and knowledgeable leader. A good shepherd offers protection, refreshment, and direction. David confidently declared that God was like a good shepherd, and he lacked nothing under God's watchful care.

You make the choice to walk in righteousness, but God establishes your path and helps you every step of the way. When you stumble, he brings restoration. When you get lost, he shows you the way. You will find peace and contentment when you follow him and submit to his watchful gaze.

How are you and your spouse trusting in your Shepherd today?

SLEEP WELL

It is in vain that you rise up early and go late to rest,
eating the bread of anxious toil;
for he gives to his beloved sleep.

PSALM 127:2 ESV

There is no holiness in overworking ourselves. God does not ask us to work to the point of exhaustion or burn out. He isn't more glorified when we are more tired. In fact, acknowledging our frailty and physical limitations leaves room for his strength to be magnified. He is so proud when we work for his glory, and he is so proud when we rest with confidence in his ability over our own.

Don't beat yourself up for needing rest. Close your eyes in peace and trust that God is in control. Give him leadership over your life and he will handle the things that you cannot. Cast your worries upon him and give him a chance to take care of them. Practice opening your hands and allowing him to take your burdens from you.

What are some practical ways you and your spouse can find rest together?

INVESTMENTS

May mercy, peace, and love be multiplied to you.

JUDE 1:2 NASB

Our investments always pay out. If we invest in the world, we will reap its flavorless fruit. If we invest in our marriage, it will be stronger and more fulfilling. If we invest in our kids, they will have a more solid foundation as adults. If we invest in God and in understanding his Word, we will reap his rewards.

God's rewards are well worth the investment he asks of you. Give him your life and he will give you an abundance of mercy, peace, and love. Offer him your talents and abilities and he will use them for his glory. Surrender your sin and he will make your heart new. Everything you give to God gets returned to you with higher value.

In what areas of life are you investing the most, and do those investments have eternal or temporary gains?

TRANSPARENCY

Search me, O God, and know my heart;
test me and know my anxious thoughts.

PSALM 139:23 NLT

We can bring our sins and fears to God, and they won't overwhelm or surprise him. In fact, he already knows about them and loves us unconditionally. He never gives up on us, and he doesn't want us to give up either. He knows the best way to conquer the sin and darkness in our life is to expose it. It's scary, uncomfortable, and humiliating, but darkness cannot exist in the light.

Bring your anxious thoughts, hidden sins, and secret struggles to the foot of the cross. Lay them down, and don't pick them back up again. Be open and honest with your spouse and be humble and contrite before the Lord. Offer him your heart and allow him to transform it.

When did you last offer your anxious heart to God?

ALL WE ARE

"Love the Lord your God with all your heart and with all your soul and with all your strength."

Deuteronomy 6:5 NIV

The Lord has never been interested in a transactional relationship with his people. He has no desire to be one of our hobbies. He deserves our full attention and passion. Loving our spouses can help us understand the way that God wants us to love him. If we long to be the sole object of our partner's affection, we can only imagine how God feels about us.

The Lord asks that our every facet be devoted to him. Our relationship with him should be lively. Much like marriage, this relationship requires effort. It demands intentionality, honesty, and humility. To love God, and to love a spouse, means loving them with all that we are emotionally, spiritually, and physically.

How can you prioritize your relationship with God this week?

PURSUED BY LOVE

Only goodness and faithful love will pursue me
all the days of my life,
and I will dwell in the house of the LORD
as long as I live.

PSALM 23:6 CSB

God's love surrounds and protects us. He is dependable, consistent, and loving, and that will never change. We do not need to fear the future because his faithfulness is proven. We have seen the way the Almighty cared for his people in the past, and we know the future is in his hands. His character is both trustworthy and constant, so our faith is sure.

Even after your life ends, God continues to take care of you and has prepared an eternal home for you within his kingdom. You are safe with him even when the world is in turmoil and you are surrounded by chaos. If you are following him, your place at this table is secure no matter what your days on earth look like.

How can you and your spouse rest in God's immovable character?

SHARPENING IRON

Iron sharpens iron,
So one man sharpens another.

PROVERBS 27:17 NASB

God didn't create us for loneliness and isolation. We need each other to work through the weaknesses in our faith. Without trusted friends to provide us with advice, encouragement, and warnings, we are left to our own interpretations and perspectives. Our spouses can offer us valuable wisdom because they sometimes see what we cannot. They are gifts from God, and the more we embrace this gift with humility the more we will benefit from it.

Be persistent in your friendship with your spouse. You will surely have uncomfortable situations come up, but don't give up. Learn how to love each other through trials and frustrations. Practice healthy conflict management and refuse to leave each other alone. There is so much goodness to be found in building each other up even when it's difficult.

How do you and your spouse regularly support and encourage each other?

UNLIMITED FORGIVENESS

"He arose and came to his father. But when he was still a great way off, his father saw him and had compassion, and ran and fell on his neck and kissed him."

LUKE 15:20 NKJV

We are God's children; we are his beloved creation. He extends compassion and love even when we fall short. His kindness is beyond our comprehension, and he upholds his faithfulness even when we do not. His love is not dependent on our virtue; he loves us because that is his character, and he has chosen us to be the recipients.

There may be times in your life when you fail to represent your Father and wander off his path. God will not give up on you in those seasons. In fact, you may even walk away with a greater sense of God's compassion and kindness. His love for you is greater than your ability to return it to him. You are never too far away for your Father's love to reach you. If you go to him in repentance, he promises to receive you with open arms and celebration.

Is there someone you need to forgive? Is there something you need to ask God's forgiveness for?

GENUINE LOVE

Let love be genuine. Abhor what is evil; hold fast to what is good.

ROMANS 12:9 ESV

The devil works hard to make sin seem attractive, but if we really understood how deeply hurtful it is to our loving God, we would abhor it. People everywhere try to romanticize their sin to appease their guilt, but the truth is that whatever is not for God is against God. Scripture tells us to hold fast to what is good because it is not easy. It takes intentionality and dedication.

To genuinely love God, you have to genuinely know God because how can you love someone you don't know? Spend time with him and learn about his character. Read the Word and cultivate love for the truth. Ask God to give you wisdom and understanding and he won't hold back.

How can you further cultivate a love for what is good?

PRAYERFUL APPROACH

Be anxious for nothing, but in everything by prayer and supplication, with thanksgiving, let your requests be made known to God; and the peace of God, which surpasses all understanding, will guard your hearts and minds through Christ Jesus.

PHILIPPIANS 4:6-7 NKJV

Christian marriage is not devoid of problems, but the difference is we can take issues to Christ in prayer and find help. Instead of feeling anxious and overwhelmed, believers may humbly and gratefully approach God with whatever is on their minds.

It's not likely you have a problem free marriage. You are just as human as the next person, and you and your spouse are not exempt from suffering. The way you deal with failures and trials is far more important than how many of them you have. Remember that you can make all your requests known to God. Develop the habit of giving him your problems the moment they arise. Reliance on Christ creates deeper contentment and peace than a lack of conflict ever could.

How do you and your spouse typically handle trials?

THE GREATEST LOVE

"Greater love has no one than this, than to lay down one's life for his friends."

JOHN 15:13 NKJV

Christ loved and cherished the church so dearly that he gave up his life for her. In doing so, he offered the greatest example of love. He taught us that there is nothing greater than an innocent person willingly sacrificing themselves for someone who is guilty.

Love is a lifestyle that goes far beyond feelings or empty words. Every day Jesus served those he met. He washed feet, fed people who were hungry, healed the hurt, and taught those who were desperate to understand more. If your love isn't backed up by actions it might be time to re-evaluate your heart. It might feel unnerving but ask your spouse if they have felt loved by your actions lately.

What specific actions make you and your spouse feel loved?

CONFIDENCE IN GOD

Do not throw away this confident trust in the Lord. Remember the great reward it brings you! Patient endurance is what you need now, so that you will continue to do God's will. Then you will receive all that he has promised.

HEBREWS 10:35-36 NLT

It's tempting to rely on our abilities and resources rather than trust the Lord and depend on his provisions, but we can't serve two masters. It is either us or God. Scripture constantly reminds us to place our trust in the Lord because it turns out much better for us if we do. We can keep pressing on against all odds because we have confidence in God's ability and intention to provide for us.

You can face today's challenges with courage and confidence. It may take longer than feels comfortable for things to turn around, but with patience and endurance, you will experience the rewards God has promised for those who persevere. Keep your eyes on him and remember that he always keeps his promises.

How can you and your partner grow in confidence in the midst of your current trials?

HOPE

Be of good courage,
And He shall strengthen your heart,
All you who hope in the LORD.

PSALM 31:24 NKJV

We are not like the world which only hopes in itself. We put our hope in the everlasting, all-powerful King of the universe! Our hope will never be disappointed. The Lord gives us strength and courage to face anything that comes our way.

What happens when hard times fall on you, your family, or your nation? How do you conduct yourself? If you look around, you will see people who crumble under pressure. You will see people who hide away from uncertainty, become angry and uncontrollable when threatened, or turn to temporary comfort when subjected to discomfort. God offers you another way. He reminds you to keep your chin up and your eyes on him. He assures you that he will see you through whatever comes your way.

How has God helped you persevere in the past?

GENTLE RAIN

> *"Let my teaching fall on you like rain;*
> *let my speech settle like dew.*
> *Let my words fall like rain on tender grass,*
> *like gentle showers on young plants."*
>
> DEUTERONOMY 32:2 NLT

God's expectation is not that we comprehend everything instantly but that we follow him into maturity. His words are refreshing to our thirsty hearts; they are like a drink of cool water when we are weary. His revelations offer us hope during hard times, and his promises encourage us when we are down. It is by his words that we mature and through his lessons that we grow stronger.

Think of how the world feels fresh after a spring rain. Everything seems new and the promise of new life is energizing. God's teaching has the same impact on your heart. Run to him and let him refresh you. Give him your burdens and let him give you new life. Don't stumble through the desert when God offers you the promise of his Word to refresh your thirsty soul.

Which of the Lord's lessons have you been grappling with lately?

CHOOSE KINDNESS

Never let loyalty and kindness leave you!
Tie them around your neck as a reminder.
Write them deep within your heart.

PROVERBS 3:3 NLT

Anyone can be loyal and kind when it's mutually beneficial and life is good. The real challenge is choosing kindness when we are angry, frustrated, or stressed out. God's call to kindness isn't exclusive to seasons of ease. He asks us to write kindness deep within our hearts so that when trials come we are not depleted. He knows that undeserved kindness has an incredible impact on whoever receives it.

There are so many ways you can choose to be kind to your spouse. Pay attention to their wants and needs. Do they love it when the house is clean? Take some extra time to put away clutter. Do they feel cared for when the snow is wiped off their windshield? Wake up a few minutes early and do it for them. Do they come alive when you compliment their appearance? Go out of your way to tell them what you think is beautiful about them. If you take time to think about it, you can come up with a multitude of ways to be kind.

What are some practical ways you can show kindness to your husband or wife?

NO PLAN B

"You will seek Me and find Me
when you search for Me with all your heart."

JEREMIAH 29:13 NASB

When we get married we assume that we are our spouse's first choice. Most people don't enter into marriage knowing that they are someone's plan B. We all long to be prioritized, valued, and put first. We all want to be deliberately chosen, well-liked, and intimately loved.

God is no different. He has no intention of being anyone's plan B or sharing his throne with other gods in your life. There is no room for half-hearted Christians in his perfect plan. Humbly and sincerely, lay your other dreams and gods down before him and search for him with your whole heart.

Are there areas of your life that you've given to God half-heartedly?

PRINCE OF PEACE

God showed how much he loved us by sending his one and only Son into the world so that we might have eternal life through him.

1 John 4:9 NLT

Christmas is a holiday associated with peace. We know this in theory, but our culture doesn't do a particularly good job of putting this idea into practice. If we look around at commercialism and worldly influences, Christmas seems to be a holiday of anxiety, greed, and discontentment. There isn't a lot of peace to be found.

As God's child, your allegiance is to the Prince of Peace. Drown out the chaos of the world and remember what Jesus has done for you. He stepped away from the perfection of heaven and humbly walked the earth. He embraced a life of suffering so that you could have eternal life. Offer him your heartfelt praise this Christmas season and refuse to be consumed by the ways of the world.

How can you and your spouse embrace peace this Christmas season?

THE MESSIAH

"Today in the town of David a Savior has been born to you; he is the Messiah, the Lord."

Luke 2:11 NIV

The Lord Almighty did not owe us salvation. There was no requirement for him to take on humanity, subject himself to the miseries of life and death, and become the perfect atonement for our sins. Not only was he willing to undergo all of this, but he did so with great joy because he knew that the outcome would be our freedom. His love for us is beyond measure!

The manner in which he was born, lived, and died demonstrated greatest humility and deep love. The world expected a conquering king, yet he showed up as a selfless servant. There is no way to fathom or explain a love like this; we can only choose to gratefully accept it and pronounce him Lord and Messiah.

How does Christ's sacrifice and humility impact the way you love your spouse?

CONSIDER THE CREATOR

When I consider Your heavens, the work of Your fingers,
The moon and the stars, which you have ordained,
What is man that You are mindful of him,
And the son of man that You visit him?

PSALM 8:3-4 NKJV

Nature is filled with the glory of God. Everywhere we look there is evidence of God's creativity, intelligence, and thoughtfulness. He carefully made each piece of creation fit together seamlessly. From the intricacies of a spider web to the complexity of how the moon impacts the ocean's tide, creation is a display of God's incredible work.

If God took such incredible care in making the earth, imagine how much more he cares for you. Don't marvel at a waterfall but fail to notice that you are also his masterpiece. He has done great and mighty things, and he is filled with affection for you. Take time today to soak in the miracle of God's mindfulness toward you.

When you consider your marriage and how wonderful it is, do you consider the one who created it and brought you together?

FOUNDATION

"From the beginning I told you what would happen in the end. A long time ago I told you things that have not yet happened. When I plan something, it happens. What I want to do, I will do."

ISAIAH 46:10 NCV

God does not ask us to have blind faith. In fact, he encourages us to question and test all things which we have been taught because he knows he will pass every test. Following our Maker means that we can confidently march into an unknown future and obey his directions even when they do not make sense to us because we know that he is faithful and good.

God's intentions are not a secret. His plan has been revealed from beginning to end. We might not know all the intricate details, but the overarching story is clear. God Almighty longs to be fully reconciled with his people. Everything he does comes from a foundation of love, and we know that in the end Christ will rule and reign on the earth. In the end, we will experience the perfection of God's presence forever.

What do you think was God's purpose in revealing his plan to his children?

THE EXTRA MILE

"If someone slaps you on one cheek, turn to them the other also. If someone takes your coat, do not withhold your shirt from them. Give to everyone who asks you, and if anyone takes what belongs to you, do not demand it back. Do to others as you would have them do to you."

LUKE 6:29-31 NIV

This passage appears counterproductive or even dangerous at face value. Who wants to turn the other cheek when slapped? Most of us would feel the urge to retaliate. The point Jesus was making wasn't to allow ourselves to be abused or become a passive participant in violence; it's about going the extra mile.

As a follower of Jesus, you are called to go above and beyond what is expected of you because that is how Jesus lived. In marriage, you will face times when you must go the extra mile, not because you are forced, but because of your great love and devotion for Jesus.

How have you experienced your spouse going the extra mile for you, and how did their sacrificial love impact you?

LIVING FOR GOD

God is not unjust; he will not forget your work and the love you have shown him as you have helped his people and continue to help them.

HEBREWS 6:10 NIV

We love God when we choose to love others. Each small act of kindness counts. God sees what we do even if the recipient doesn't notice or never says thank you. Today's Scripture is encouraging because it is a reminder that nothing is wasted in God's kingdom.

Marriage is filled with seemingly insignificant acts of kindness. Every little sacrifice you made is seen by God. He is aware of you each time you hold your tongue, wipe up a mess, or work diligently when you don't want to. Everything you do in his name will be rewarded. He promises not to forget you.

How can you shift your mindset from longing for your spouse's approval to being satisfied with God's acknowledgement?

LED BY GOD

I praise the Lord because he advises me.
Even at night, I feel his leading.
I keep the Lord before me always.
Because he is close by my side,
I will not be hurt.

Psalm 16:7-8 NCV

It is difficult to live without direction, purpose, or instruction. Like a ship on the ocean without any control, we would be hopelessly lost without God's Word to guide us. If we did not have the counsel of the Scriptures to save us from the devil's schemes and the world's wickedness, we would veer off in the wrong direction and be dashed upon the rocks.

This psalm offers reassurance that if you stay with the Lord, you will not be overcome when the waves begin to crash. Troubles will come, but you can also be certain that God will be with you in those moments. You have nothing to fear if you keep him before you. Holding fast to him is the safest place you can be, especially in a world that is chaotic and confusing.

As you and your spouse prepare for this coming year, have you asked God to go before you?

CHRIST WITHIN

Him we proclaim, warning everyone and teaching everyone with all wisdom, that we may present everyone mature in Christ. For this I toil, struggling with all his energy that he powerfully works within me.

COLOSSIANS 1:28-29 ESV

When Jesus Christ takes up residence in our hearts, he brings new desires, principles, motives, and goals with him. His transforming presence reshapes us, and our lives take on new meaning. He becomes the source of power for our marriages, jobs, ambitions, ministries, and friendships. We become shining lights on a hill for all who are lost in darkness.

A Christ-centered marriage is a powerful force for good in a world where selfishness reigns supreme. The way you treat your spouse puts God's love on display. As you mature in your relationship with God, your ability to love others should expand. If love is not the fruit of your maturity, it might be time to ask yourself what you are toiling for.

In what areas can you mature in love?